USA
NASA
Challenger

THE OMSI COOKBOOK

OREGON MUSEUM OF SCIENCE AND INDUSTRY

Leslie J. Whipple

— *A Maverick Publication* —

ISBN 0-89288-244-1

Cover Food Photography, Design and Photo Composition—Stephen Ingham

Food Stylist—Leslie J. Whipple

Layout and Design—Bridget R. Wise

Cover Photo of OMSI Building—Rob Hoffman

Additional Writers—Pat Janowski

To order ***The OMSI Cookbook***, contact Maverick Distributors at
Drawer 7289, Bend, Oregon 97708
1-800-333-8046

■

To Jerry,
for changing my destiny.

■

▪ ACKNOWLEDGMENTS ▪

I would like to express my gratitude and appreciation to Jerry Crowley who made everything possible.

I also wish to thank:

Stewart M. Whipple
Marcia J. Whipple
Stephen Ingham
Dotti Wilson
Marilynne Eichinger
David Heil
Michelle Marquart
Terry Hiller
Helen Hall
Gary Asher
Tom Healy
Bridget Wise
H. Bruce Miller

This book would not have been possible without the contributions and cooperation of many people, especially the staff of OMSI, who made their recipes, stories and expertise available to *The OMSI Cookbook.* I wish to thank them all for their generosity.

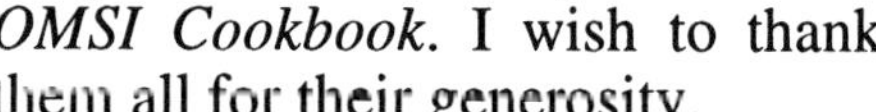

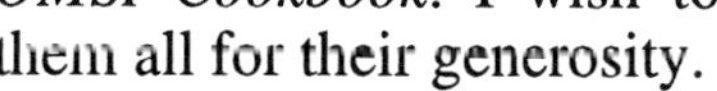

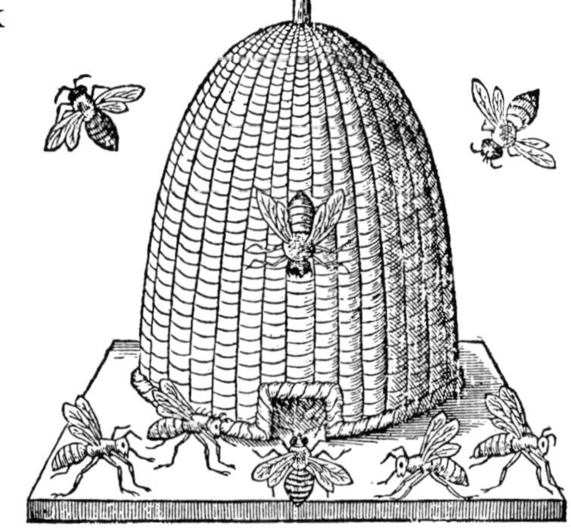

▪ TABLE OF CONTENTS ▪

The original OMSI building on Hassalo Street.

▪ OMSI'S MISSION STATEMENT ▪

The Oregon Museum of Science and Industry is an independent scientific, educational, and cultural resource center dedicated to improving the public's understanding of science and technology. OMSI makes science and technology exciting and relevant through exhibits, programs, and experiences that emphasize hands-on participation.

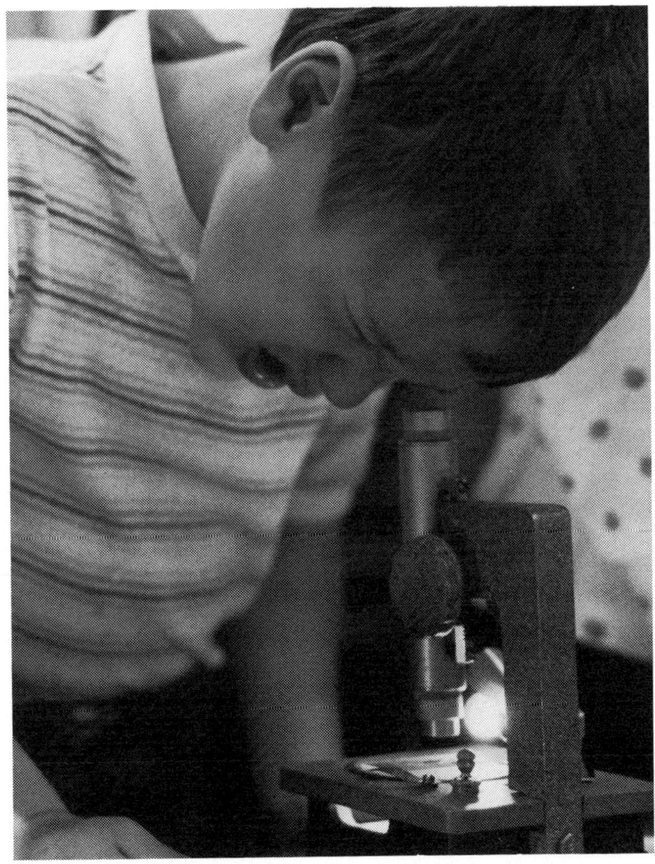

▪ INTRODUCTION TO *The OMSI Cookbook* ▪

I have always believed that "the family that eats together stays together." As a result, at our house the dinner hour has become a time of sharing and caring, not only about food but about personal well being.

In my family cooking is an exercise in experimentation. It was very difficult for me to write down my favorite recipes because they are ever-changing depending on the weather, my purse, and my mood. My husband, Marty, is an expert at leftovers. He has a knack for combining the most unusual flavors and producing a visual and gastronomic masterpiece. His downfall is that this gourmet delight can never be repeated. He neither remembers nor pays attention to what is being blended, but rather depends on experience, taste buds, and love of trial and error. Every once in a while he comes up with a horrid concoction and all we can do is "grin and bear it." However, the laughs make it worthwhile.

My son, Talik, has become an expert at making shakes. He combines milk, bananas, fruit juices, non-alcoholic mixes and vegetables into a shake that he appreciates. As dutiful parents, we taste, suggest, hmm and ahh, and encourage him in his deliberations. Our chemist/experimenter has been expanding his palate and is now willing to try a broader range of foods. His appreciation of science as fun, is also enhanced by his ability to play in the kitchen. Although he puts all of the foods he likes together into his shakes, he has learned that the combinations do not necessarily produce a positive result. However, when he combines an ingredient he does not like by itself with other ingredients, he at times finds he enjoys the final product.

Marilynne Eichinger, OMSI President

My specialty is the fast feast. I love to come home at the end of a hurried day and enter my kitchen with the goal of producing a masterpiece in twenty or thirty minutes. I count the steps between cabinets, table, refrigerator and sink trying to determine the most efficient way of setting the table, getting ingredients together, cooking and cleaning up.

When planning for company my process is different, with the ultimate goal of being ready for guests at least two hours before they arrive. I always rest, take a long glorious bath, and read a book before entertaining. To be able to achieve this level of luxury I start the day before by completing my shopping, cleaning and often table setting. On the day of the event I can concentrate on cooking alone and enjoy this singular task.

The dinner hour, whether with family or friends, is a time of camaraderie, relaxation and renewal. The cook's job is not only one of making good food, but of creating an atmosphere that is inviting. Conversation and sharing at the table can also help give children confidence and a sense of belonging.

When my children were young and both my husband and I were working, we used the time after dinner while still at the table, to discuss family difficulties and sibling and parental conflicts. A problem box was placed in the kitchen and whenever there was a conflict or personal problem it was written down on the spot and deposited in the problem box. Several times a week we emptied the box, reviewed the contents, and discussed the situations as a family. In most cases we were able to use our combined viewpoints and come to a joint decision. This exercise taught our children about democracy, gave them cognitive skills and helped them understand the boundary between their own needs and those of other family members. The problem box was also helpful in preventing a fight because the angry parties had to think about the situation, express it in writing and wait for a calm moment to discuss the problem.

All of us have tension in our lives. We worry about money, our jobs, and our families. What better way to relax and share than to play with a meal and present it to our family or friends who care and encourage us with both our successes and failures. Cooking, sewing and eating can be a training ground for life-long interpersonal relationships.

Marilynne Eichinger
President, OMSI

▪ Development Department ▪

Thank You! Thank You! Thank you!

OMSI's fund-raising success has been realized because of community support and volunteers.

OMSI started small—a dream and vision of the late J. C. Stevens. Our first home was the reading room of the Portland Hotel. From there it expanded to a house on Hassalo Street (now Lloyd Center); more community leaders bought into the vision of OMSI and it moved to Washington Park where the shell of the building was constructed in an old-fashioned "Barn-raising" all in one day.

OMSI has become a leader in the science museum world as a "hands-on" science education facility and renowned for its exhibit design and production. In keeping with the advancements around us, OMSI has answered the challenge by building a new facility in downtown Portland.

But the recipe never changes—it is our volunteers giving of their time and financial support—CEO's, middle management and grassroots efforts that keep OMSI in the forefront of the science education field.

Dotti Wilson
Vice President of Development

▪ The New OMSI Building ▪

Construction of the new, 219,000 square foot Oregon Museum of Science and Industry began in February, 1991, on a riverfront site along the east bank of the Willamette River in downtown Portland, Oregon. The Portland architectural firm of Zimmer Gunsul Frasca Partnership designed the new museum and surrounding grounds. Robert Frasca, who designed the Oregon Convention Center and other Portland landmarks, led the team.

Incorporated into the building's design are several geometric shapes, which echo fundamental shapes in nature and science. These features include a bright, copper-covered dome over the OMNIMAX Theater; a glazed atrium building with a pyramid-shaped top; a cylindrical-topped Sky Theater building; and a 120-foot tall, bright red smokestack.

The 18.5-acre site, formerly an historic electricity generation plant, was donated by Portland General Electrical Company. The historic, 1910-vintage turbine powerhouse structure was retained and incorporated into the new museum campus as an exhibit area. One of the building's existing steam turbines was left standing, and was refurbished as an exhibit itself, linking energy technology of the past with OMSI's state-of-the-art energy system.

APPETIZERS

▪ Traveling Exhibits ▪

OMSI's talented Design and Shop crews collaborate to produce much of what visitors see in the museum's exhibit halls. However, many museum guests may not know that OMSI also creates exhibits that travel around the country and into Canada, appearing at science centers thousands of miles from Portland. These may include large exhibitions that originally appeared at OMSI, such as Super Heroes®, Bugs Eye View and Star Trek: Federation Science™, which is now on its way to the first stop on a three-year international tour. Other, smaller exhibits can be set up in schools and libraries. Some of these are: Brain Teasers, mind benders such as tying and untying unusual knots and solving intriguing number games; the sophisticated Light & Color, where visitors can view holograms and bend laser beams; and Discover E (engineering), which features a computer-aided bridge design program and a groundwater flow simulation.

▪ CARPACCIO ANTICA POSTA ▪

BEEF TENDERLOIN ACCOMPANIED BY ARUGULA LEAVES, CELERY AND AIOLI

1 pound beef tenderloin, very fresh
1 bunch arugula, washed and dried
4 stalks celery, strings removed and minced
Cracked black peppercorns

Aioli:

16 cloves garlic
1½ teaspoons salt
3 whole eggs, very fresh, at room temperature
¼ cup fresh lemon juice
¾ cup olive oil
½ cup extra virgin olive oil
3 tablespoons boiling water
Additional lemon juice to taste

Place beef in the freezer for 15 to 30 minutes. It should be firm enough to slice thinly. Use a very sharp knife or slicer and slice ⅛-inch thick. Keep sliced beef tightly covered with plastic wrap in the refrigerator. Slice beef late in the afternoon and only enough to serve that evening.

For the Aioli: Mash garlic and salt together with a mortar and pestle until it forms a smooth paste. Set aside. Put eggs and lemon juice in the bowl of a food processor. Pulse to blend. Combine olive oils in a pitcher or measuring cup. With processor running, add oil in a thin, steady stream to the egg mixture. When mayonnaise emulsifies, add oil more quickly to make a thin mayonnaise. Turn off machine and add garlic paste, boiling water and more lemon juice. Pulse to blend. It should be fairly thin. Add cold water if necessary.

Arrange beef on plate with arugula and celery. Drizzle with Aioli and cracked black peppercorns. Serves 6 to 8.

Catherine Whims
Joan Husman
Genoa
Portland, Oregon

Your Pal "Omsi"

In 1957 a cartoon imp from outer space named "Omsi" was created by Robert Welch and designed by former Walt Disney artist Moe Martindale. This enticing little creature, with a 'telerossiter' antenna perched on his domed head, pied pipered the children of Oregon into calling BElmont 2-2156 to receive his personally telephoned secret message as to where they could get one of his 50,000 "Magic OMSI keys" to science and industry that would entitle them to his personally autographed pictures! They so completely jammed Portland's communication system to the East Side police and fire departments that announcements had to be made on the radio, TV, and in the newspapers, NOT to call his telephone number! On February 18, 1957, it seemed all the children in Portland and the surrounding areas were downtown to see for themselves the outer space man "Omsi" in the Meier & Frank Company store window.

▪ WINGS OF FIRE ▪

These chicken wings are not as hot as you would think. Everyone loves them----they are almost addictive.

1 cup Tabasco sauce
⅓ cup brown sugar
¼ cup cider vinegar
4 pounds chicken drumettes **OR** wings

Preheat oven to 350 degrees.

Combine Tabasco, brown sugar and vinegar in a glass or other non-reactive baking pan, and whisk until smooth. Add chicken and marinate overnight, turning occasionally.

Bake wings for about 1 hour, or until very tender. Chicken can also be grilled.

Jerry Crowley

▪ MARINATED HORS D'OEUVRES ▪

8 ounces Mozzarella cheese, cut into ½-inch cubes
8 ounces cooked ham, cut into ½-inch cubes
24 cherry tomatoes
24 ripe olives
12 small mushrooms
1 14-ounce can artichoke hearts, drained

Marinade:

⅓ cup red wine vinegar
2 cloves garlic, minced
1 teaspoon basil
1 teaspoon dry mustard
1 teaspoon thyme
1 teaspoon seasoned salt
½ teaspoon oregano
¼ teaspoon black pepper, freshly ground
1 cup salad or olive oil

Arrange Mozzarella, ham, cherry tomatoes, olives, mushrooms and artichoke hearts on skewers. Combine marinade ingredients and whisk to blend well. Marinate skewers overnight, turning occasionally.

Carolyn Rose

▪ CARROT CRUDITE ▪

A refreshing, no-fat nibble with cocktails.

6 carrots, peeled
Juice of 1 lemon
Salt to taste

Slice carrots at and angle. Place in a jar with a lid. Add lemon juice and salt to taste. Cover with lid and shake gently to distribute seasonings. Refrigerate until thoroughly chilled. Serve on a bed of ice.

Mrs. Donald W. (Gretchen) Fraser

▪ KILLER SALSA ▪

3 pounds Roma tomatoes, chopped
3 to 4 Serrano chilies, seeded and minced
2 jalapeno chilies, seeded and minced
1 green bell pepper, chopped
1 small onion, chopped
¼ cup fresh cilantro, minced
¼ cup fresh parsley, minced
¼ cup lemon juice
1 tablespoon cider vinegar
1 teaspoon cumin

Combine all ingredients in a blender and puree until smooth. Cover and chill for 3 hours to allow flavors to develop. Serve as a dip with tortilla chips, or as an accompaniment to Mexican food.

Stewart M. Whipple, Jr.

▪ CURRIED CHICKEN SPREAD ▪

1 cup poached chicken (skin removed), diced
¼ cup celery, minced
2 tablespoons green onion, minced
2 tablespoons toasted almonds, finely chopped (optional)
2 tablespoons low-fat sour cream
2 tablespoons low-fat mayonnaise
1 teaspoon curry powder
1 teaspoon fresh lemon juice
¼ teaspoon salt

Combine all ingredients in a medium bowl, or mix in a food processor or blender until smooth. Chill. Serve with crackers, toast or fill mini pita bread halves. Makes approximately 1½ cups.

Jim and Karen Bosley

▪ HOT ARTICHOKE DIP ▪

This is an easy appetizer and can easily be put together from items in the pantry.

1 14-ounce can artichokes, drained and chopped
1 4-ounce can chopped green chilies, drained
1 cup mayonnaise
1 cup Parmesan cheese
Paprika

Preheat oven to 350 degrees.

In a large bowl, combine artichokes, chilies, mayonnaise and Parmesan and mix well. Place mixture in a baking dish and sprinkle top with paprika. Bake for 20 minutes, or until hot and bubbly. Serve with slices of French bread, crackers or tortilla chips.

Mary Anne Nance

▪ CHICKEN NACHOS ▪

2 cups cooked chicken **OR** turkey, cubed
¾ cup water
1 package Lawry's taco seasoning mix
1 16-ounce can refried beans
Tortilla chips
Cheddar cheese, grated
Black olives, sliced
Green onions, sliced
Tomatoes, chopped
Salsa
Sour cream
Guacamole

In a medium saucepan, combine chicken, water and taco seasoning. Simmer over medium-low heat until all of the water has evaporated. Set aside.

On a microwave-safe platter, spread the refried beans. Stick the tortilla chips into the beans in a decorative pattern. Top with the prepared chicken, cheese, olives, green onions and tomatoes. Microwave until hot and cheese is melted. Top with sour cream and guacamole. Enjoy!

Senator Bob Packwood

▪ CHALET SWISS FONDUE ▪

One of the most popular fondue customs is that if a lady loses her bread cube in the fondue, she owes the man on her right a kiss. If a man has such a mishap when dining in a restaurant, he should buy the next round of drinks. At home, he owes his hostess a kiss.

As seen on the television show, "Live with Regis and Kathy Lee."

1 clove garlic, lightly crushed
10 ounces Swiss Emmental, finely grated
10 ounces Swiss Gruyere, finely grated
4 teaspoons cornstarch
2 cups dry white wine
1 tablespoon lemon juice
¼ cup Kirsch **OR** Eau-de-Vie
¼ teaspoon freshly ground black pepper
¼ teaspoon freshly ground nutmeg
2 loaves crusty Italian or French bread, cut into 1-inch cubes
Assorted raw vegetables such as mushrooms, cherry tomatoes, cauliflower, broccoli florets, celery and carrots (optional)

Rub the inside of a medium saucepan with the clove of garlic, then discard garlic. Place the grated cheeses in the saucepan and add the cornstarch. Add the wine and lemon juice and stir. Turn the heat to high and cook, stirring constantly, until fondue is smooth and creamy. Reduce heat to low and stir in Kirsch, pepper and nutmeg. Cook for about 3 minutes, stirring constantly.

Transfer fondue to a fondue pot. Adjust flame of burner under fondue pot so fondue continues bubbling very lightly. Serve each guest bread cubes from a plate or a basket. Spear fork through soft part of bread first, securing prongs in crust. Dunk to bottom and stir well. Remove fork and twist over pot to break threads of fondue.

Kurt Mezger
Chalet Swiss Specialty Restaurant
Welches, Oregon

▪ A GARLIC LOVER'S TREAT ▪

This is a wonderful cold weather starter for eight people or two garlic lovers. A wonderful beginning to a leg of lamb dinner. Serve with a dry full-bodied Oregon Riesling or Gewurtztraminer.

6 tablespoons olive oil
6 tablespoons unsalted butter
50 cloves of garlic, unpeeled
1½ cups Amity Estate Dry Riesling **OR** Amity Gewurtztraminer
Freshly ground pepper to taste
8 slices toasted bread
8 tablespoons fresh basil **OR** parsley **OR** chives, minced

Heat oil and butter in a heavy skillet and sauté the garlic over medium-low heat for 5 minutes. Add wine and pepper and simmer, uncovered, for 15 minutes. When garlic is very tender, remove with a slotted spoon, and squeeze out the garlic cloves. Discard garlic peels. Transfer cooked garlic to a blender or food processor and blend into a paste. Increase heat under skillet to medium and reduce wine sauce by half.

Spread garlic paste over toast and top with wine sauce. Sprinkle with 1 tablespoon basil.

Vikki Wetle

▪ MINTED AVOCADO SALSA ▪

1 avocado, firm but ripe; peeled, pitted and diced into ¼-inch chunks
1 small tomato; peeled, seeded and diced
3 tablespoons fresh mint, minced
6 tablespoons olive oil
4 tablespoons rice wine vinegar
1 teaspoon chili powder
1 teaspoon cumin
1 teaspoon salt

Combine all ingredients and mix thoroughly. Makes approximately 1½ cups.

Jake's Seafood Cookbook

▪ PAPAYA-CHILI SALSA ▪

1 papaya, firm but ripe; peeled, seeded and diced into ¼-inch chunks
1 small jalapeno, seeded and minced
1 tablespoon fresh mint, minced
1 tablespoon red onion, finely minced
1 teaspoon cumin
Pinch chili powder
2 tablespoons rice wine vinegar
1 tablespoon olive oil

Combine all ingredients and mix thoroughly. Makes approximately 1½ cups.

Jake's Seafood Cookbook

▪ ORANGE AND GINGER SPARERIBS ▪

3 pounds spareribs, cut into 2-inch pieces by your butcher

Marinade:

5 teaspoons soy sauce
2 tablespoons fresh orange juice
1 tablespoon rice vinegar
2 teaspoons fresh ginger, minced
2 teaspoons orange zest, minced
3 tablespoons cornstarch
1½ tablespoons sugar

Glaze:

4 tablespoons fresh orange juice
4 tablespoons soy sauce
3 tablespoons sugar
1 tablespoon rice vinegar

In a large stainless steel, or other non-reactive, bowl, combine soy sauce, orange juice, vinegar, ginger and orange zest. Stir together cornstarch and sugar and whisk into soy sauce mixture. Add spareribs and stir to coat well. Cover and refrigerate overnight, stirring occasionally.

Remove spareribs from marinade and place in heat-proof pans or dishes (cake pans work well). Place pans in a large pot with a steaming rack. Cover tightly and bring to a boil. Reduce heat to medium-low and steam for 40 minutes. Remove from steamer and drain spareribs in a colander.

Preheat oven to 350 degrees. Lightly oil a 9-inch by 13-inch baking dish.

Place drained spareribs in a single layer in prepared baking dish. Combine glaze ingredients and pour over spareribs. Bake for 20 minutes. Turn spareribs over and bake an additional 20 minutes.

Leslie J. Whipple

▪ FRESH SALSA ▪

Fresh salsas, once exclusively associated with Mexican cuisine, are the ideal accompaniment for many varieties of grilled seafood. All of the chefs in our company have lent their creativity to developing these light and flavorful salsas. Once you try the basic recipe and a couple of variations, you just might be inspired to create some salsas of your own.

1 cup tomatoes; peeled, seeded and chopped
⅓ cup red onion, diced
½ cup bell peppers; red, green or yellow, diced
2 tablespoons cilantro, minced
½ tablespoon cumin
1 teaspoon chili powder
1 teaspoon garlic, minced
¼ cup olive oil
1 tablespoon lime juice
Minced jalapeno pepper, to taste (1 for medium, 2 for hot, 3 for very hot)
1 teaspoon salt
¼ cup commercial salsa (optional) if you like your salsa to have a looser consistency

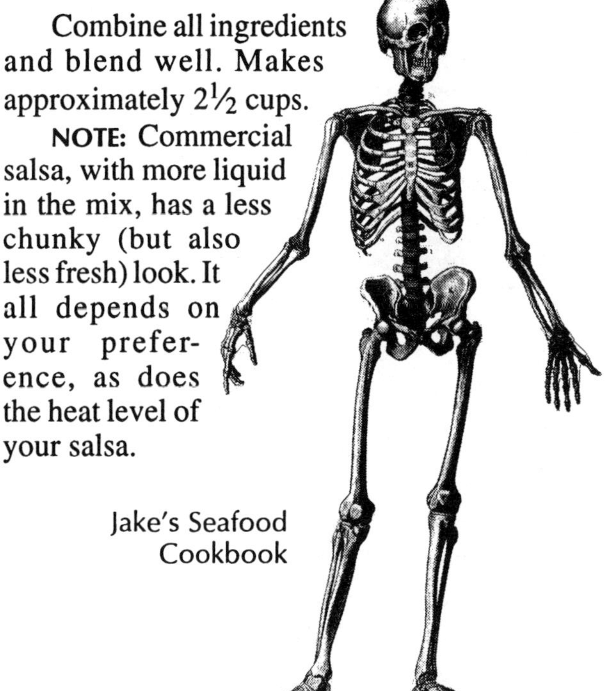

Combine all ingredients and blend well. Makes approximately 2½ cups.

NOTE: Commercial salsa, with more liquid in the mix, has a less chunky (but also less fresh) look. It all depends on your preference, as does the heat level of your salsa.

Jake's Seafood Cookbook

Martinelli's Non-Alcoholic Cocktail Recipes

These non-alcoholic cocktail recipes are the top prize winners in a Martinelli's Sparkling Cider competition.

▪ PINK PASSION FRAPPE ▪

2 ounces Martinelli's Sparkling Cider
2 ounces pineapple juice
2 ounces cranberry juice cocktail
Whipped Cream
Lime slice and cherry for garnish

Blend Martinelli's Apple Cider, pineapple juice and cranberry juice with ice. Serve in a champagne glass with a dollop of whipped cream, lime slice and cherry. Makes 1 drink.

Bret Rose, 1st Place

▪ MARTINELLI'S SPARKLER ▪

8 ounces Martinelli's Sparkling Cider
2 splashes grenadine
Splash of Rose's Lime Juice
Lemon slice and cherry for garnish

Fill highball glass with ice and add ingredients. Garnish with Lemon slice and cherry. Makes 1 drink.

Sandra Larsen, 2nd place

▪ APPLE JUICE À LA MODE ▪

8 ounces Martinelli's Sparkling Cider
1 scoop vanilla ice cream
Cinnamon to taste
Whipped cream and nutmeg for garnish

Blend Martinelli's Sparkling Cider, ice cream and cinnamon together and pour into a highball glass. Serve with a dollop of whipped cream and a sprinkle of nutmeg. Makes 1 drink.

Rick Ongaro, 3rd place

Sylvia Brown

Food for Spaceflight

After a long workday in space, astronauts like nothing better than a good dinner. Meals are as important in space as they are on Earth for both good health and relaxation. After many years of experience, NASA has developed a meal system for use on the Space Shuttle that combines a wide variety of delicious and nutritious foods with food packaging and preparation technology that makes it convenient and easy to use in space.

Space foods weren't always delicious or easy to eat. In the early days of spaceflight, Mercury astronauts squeezed processed food from aluminum toothpaste tubes and ate sandwich cubes coated with unflavored gelatin that kept breadcrumbs from making a mess in the tiny spacecraft cabins. The food, though nutritious, was not very appetizing. It lacked the look and feel that make eating pleasurable on Earth. After many experiments with food types, packaging and preparation, NASA reached an important conclusion. It was possible and safe to carry normal foods into space and eat them in an almost normal way. The big difference was how foods were packaged and prepared in orbit.

Foods for Space Shuttle astronauts come in many different forms. Some are freeze-dried while others are thermally stabilized, dried, or eaten in natural form. Thermally stabilized dinner entrees, such as beef stew or smoked turkey, are packed in foil and plastic pouches. They are heated in the Shuttle's oven and eaten when ready. Dried and freeze-dried foods are packed in special plastic food containers with flexible lids. Hot or cold water must be added to make the food ready for eating.

▪ A Typical Space Shuttle Menu ▪

DAY 1

Dried Pears (IM)
Sausage Patty (R)
Scrambled Eggs (R)
Bran Flakes (R)
Cocoa (B)
Orange-Pineapple Drink (B)

Ham (T)
Bread (NF)
Diced Peaches (T)
Pecan Cookies (NF)
Apple Drink (B)

Chicken a la King (T)
Chicken and Rice (R)
Asparagus (R)
Chocolate Pudding (T)
Grape Drink (B)

DAY 2

Dried Peaches (IM)
Granola (R)
Breakfast Roll (I) (NF)
Vanilla Instant Breakfast (B)
Orange-Grapefruit Drink (B)

Salmon (T)
Bread (NF)
Butter Cookies (NF)
Orange Drink (B)

Beef with Barbeque Sauce (T)
Potatoes au Gratin (R)
Green Beans with Mushrooms (R)
Butterscotch Pudding (T)
Orange Drink (B)

DAY 3

Dried Apricots (IM)
Seasoned Scrambled Eggs (R)
Bran Flakes (R)
Cocoa (B)
Orange Juice Mix (B)

Peanut Butter (T)
Jelly (T)
Bread (NF)
Fruit Cocktail (T)
Fruit Cake (T)
Tea with Lemon and Sugar (B)

Frankfurters (T)
Potato Patty (R)
Green Beans with Broccoli (R)
Strawberries (R)
Vanilla Pudding (T) (R)
Tropical Punch (B)

ABBREVIATIONS : T = Thermostabilized; IM = Intermediate Moisture; FD = Freeze Dried; R = Rehydratable; NF = Natural Form; B = Beverage.

▪ WELSH RAREBIT ▪

This is called 'Caws Wedi Pobi' in Welsh.

½ cup Cheddar cheese, grated
4 tablespoons milk **OR** beer
2 teaspoons Worcestershire sauce
2 teaspoons flour
1 teaspoon dry mustard
1 teaspoon butter
4 pieces of toast

Put grated cheese in a small sauce pan and place over low heat until cheese starts to melt. Add milk, Worcestershire sauce, flour, mustard and butter and whisk over low heat until smooth. Spread cheese mixture on toast and grill under a broiler until bubbly.

Ken Brace
Bryn Seion Welsh Church

The Replicating Gourmet: "DINING in the 24th CENTURY"

"COMPUTER: Tea. Earl Grey. Hot."

Imagine eating on a 24th century starship: replicator technology gives you over 4,500 virtually perfect, nutritionally correct dishes every time, you don't have to wash the dishes, and they've got synthenol that never gives you a hangover. Want to whip up your own meal? Just ask the computer for a wok and fresh endive!

Sounds great, but hold on a minute! *Just* 4,500 selections in memory? And of that 4,500, how many are Terran dishes? There are hundreds of civilizations and species, each with their own stable of prepared foods. Assuming equal menu parity among a crew representing only five civilizations, that's 900 different selections specifically for humans, or barely three different selections per day. If you have three meals a day, that works out to be a pretty boring diet, no matter how good the food is. You gotta hope you can eat Vulcan bertakk soup, whatever that is.

The language of cooking must have changed, too, for a person to give only brief instructions. The captain's standard drink request sounds straightforward enough, *providing* there's an objective temperature template for concepts such as hot, cool, tepid, cold and scalding. How many decisions—temperature and other—have to be made for that uniformly perfect "Beef Wellington, Yorkshire pudding, asparagus with Hollandaise sauce"?

More fundamentally, each dish *is* uniformly the same—a gourmet treat—but barring a computer malfunction, *always* the same. Part of the fun of cooking seems to be personalizing the dish—changing this or that to suit your taste. How much trouble would "COMPUTER: a hoagie: hold the mustard; add extra ketchup and double onions," cause?

Who decides the on-file menu, anyway, and how easy is it to make additions or changes in the memory? Are there Starfleet test kitchens that review gourmet foods around the galaxy and post candidates for inclusion? Is there a roving 24th century version of James Beard or Duncan Hines who is eating his/her/its way across the galaxy? Is there a galactic gourmet guide?

Pity poor Diana Troi. While at Starfleet Academy, she developed a taste for baker's semi-sweet chocolate, probably the only chocolate the starship replicators don't have in memory! With a 25-year mission ahead of her, I'm *sure* she'll find a way to get semi-sweet in there.

While she's at it, I know a little restaurant on the Willamette (Sol System. Earth. Nor-Am. West coast. Portland Complex. Late 20th Century, old calendar) that has the best razor clams you ever ate. Maybe she should talk to somebody at Starfleet Nutrition . . .

Terry Hiller

▪ EARL GREY TEA, HOT ▪

Put fresh, cold water in a kettle and bring to a boil. Pour about 1 cup boiling water into the teapot and return kettle to the heat. Swirl the hot water around to warm the teapot, then pour out. Put 1 teaspoon Earl Grey Tea for each cup in the pot. Pour boiling water into the teapot and put the lid on. Allow to steep for 3 to 5 minutes. Pour the tea through a strainer into cups. Serve with sugar, lemon slices and sugar.

▪ WINTER NIGHT SPECIAL ▪

(HOT MULLED WINE)

A skier friend in Colorado gave me this recipe for après-ski socializing. It's nice on a cold rainy night too.

2 quarts cranberry juice cocktail
1 quart water
2 cups sugar
4 sticks cinnamon
24 whole cloves
Rind of ½ lime
2 quarts red wine
½ cup lime juice
Nutmeg
Lime slices

In a large sauce pan, combine cranberry juice, water, cinnamon sticks, cloves and lime rind. Bring to a boil, stirring constantly. Reduce to heat to low and simmer 15 minutes. Strain and discard solids. Return cranberry juice mixture to sauce pan. Add wine and lime juice and heat to a simmer. Serve in heated mugs. Sprinkle with nutmeg and float a thin lime slice on top. Serves 24.

Susan G. Butruille, Author
Women's Voices from the Oregon Trail

▪ BRIDGETOWN ARTICHOKES ▪

I enjoy this delight year-round, but never more than in the summer when I teach OMSI "Bridge Walking and LEGO Bridge Building" for Portland-area fifth, sixth, seventh and eighth graders. Bridgetown Artichokes are a creation of my friend, Sharlene Mason.

3 artichokes
2 tablespoons olive oil
1 small clove garlic. minced
Salt and pepper to taste

Trim the tips of the artichokes. Steam until just tender. Cut in half length-wise and remove the choke. Combine olive oil and garlic and drizzle over the cut-sides of the halved artichokes. Season to taste with salt and pepper.

Bridgetown Artichokes can be served, chilled, as an appetizer or salad, or, when hot, as a vegetable side dish.

Sharon M. Wood, Author
The Portland Bridge Book

▪ CHRISTMAS CORDIAL ▪

15 to 16 Damson plums
7 cups sugar
1 liter vodka

Prepare a 1 gallon jar with a tight-fitting lid by washing jar and lid with hot, soapy water. Rinse well and set aside.

Wash and air-dry plums. Pierce each plum several times with a sharp knife. Pack the jar in layers, beginning with the plums, then sugar and finally vodka. Repeat until jar is full and the vodka completely covers the plums. Screw the lid on snugly but not fully tightened. Do not remove the lid at any time during the steeping process. Gently invert the jar several times each week to mix the cordial. Steep for 3 months. Strain the cordial into a smaller container. Discard the fruit. Damson plums are available in the autumn so the steeping process will be complete around Christmas.

Claris Poppert

▪ PUREE DI MELANZANE ALLA GORGONZOLA AL POMODORA RAGU ▪

(EGGPLANT TIMBALES WITH GORGONZOLA SAUCE AND TOMATO SAUCE)

I had a version of this wonderful dish in Siena, Italy, which I have recreated using eggplant instead of asparagus. This is a unique first course that truly exemplifies the culinary magic of Italian Cucina.

Eggplant Timbales:

5 tablespoons olive oil
1 to 2 cloves garlic, minced
1 medium eggplant, peeled and diced
1 cup heavy cream
¾ cup fresh Parmesan cheese, grated
1 egg
Salt and pepper to taste

Tomato Sauce:

⅓ cup olive oil
1 clove garlic, minced
3 pounds ripe tomatoes; peeled seeded and chopped
Salt to taste
1 tablespoon fresh basil, minced
1 tablespoon fresh Italian flat-leaf parsley, minced

Gorgonzola Sauce:

½ cup heavy cream
1 tablespoon sour cream
3 tablespoons Gorgonzola cheese, crumbled
1 tablespoon butter
Salt and pepper to taste

For the Eggplant Timbales:

Preheat oven to 375 degrees. Butter individual ¾ cup molds.

Heat the olive oil in a large skillet over medium heat. Add the garlic and sauté until fragrant. Add eggplant and sauté until golden brown, about 20 to 25 minutes. Add cream and cook for about 5 to 7 minutes, or until cream is absorbed. Transfer mixture into the bowl of a food processor and process until smooth. Add Parmesan and egg and process until smooth. Season with salt and pepper to taste. Pour ½ cup of the mixture into prepared molds and place in large pan. Add enough water to come half way up the sides of the molds. Bake for about 20 minutes or until firm.

For the Tomato Sauce:

Heat the olive oil in a large skillet over medium heat. Add garlic and sauté just until fragrant. Add tomatoes and salt to taste. Bring to a boil, then reduce heat to medium-low and simmer for about 20 minutes. Stir in basil and parsley and remove from heat.

For the Gorgonzola Sauce:

Combine all ingredients in a small sauce pan and stir over low heat until smooth.

To Serve:

Put a large spoonful of Tomato Sauce on a plate. Unmold Timbale onto Tomato Sauce. Spoon Gorgonzola Sauce on top of each Timbale.

Patricia Wied

SALADS

▪ USS Blueback Submarine Exhibit ▪

Preparations are underway for the Oregon Museum of Science and Industry to receive the USS Blueback, a 219-foot submarine which will be permanently docked in the Willamette River in the Spring of 1994. The Blueback will be the focus of exhibits covering undersea exploration, and the complex technological challenges overcome to enable humans to live and work underwater for prolonged periods.

After being formerly released from the US Navy, the Blueback will be towed from its present berth at the Puget Sound Naval Shipyard in Bremerton, Washington, up the Columbia and Willamette Rivers to a temporary berth at the Naval Reserve Center at Swan Island. Hull modifications will be made at Portland area shipyards to permit access for the public, then the sub will be moved to its final berth in the Willamette River next to OMSI. Additional internal modifications will enable visitors to explore the inside of the two-decked craft. Interpretive signs and a guided walking tour will lead visitors through the sub's narrow passageways and provide scientific, technical and historical information.

The Blueback, a diesel-electric powered submarine of the Barbel Class, was among the last of the Navy's non-nuclear submarines built. First commissioned in October, 1959, the Blueback was active in the US Navy Submarine Force of the Pacific Fleet from 1961 through 1990. Among its noteworthy achievements were setting a record for traveling 5,340 miles from Yokosuka, Japan to San Diego, California entirely submerged, and visiting the Portland Rose Festival in 1978 and 1981. More recently, the Blueback appeared in the movie, "The Hunt For Red October."

When final renovations and a public access dock are completed, the Blueback will be formally opened to the public sometime in the late Spring of 1994, as part of OMSI's 50th Birthday celebration.

▪ ASIAN SHRIMP NOODLE SALAD ▪

This salad is great served as a main dish with a crusty French bread and Gewurtztraminer.

1 12-ounce package Chinese egg noodles, cooked according to directions and rinsed in cold water
1 pound fresh bean sprouts, cut into 3-inch lengths
1 medium cucumber; peeled, seeded and sliced
2 cups broccoli flowerets, blanched and refreshed under cold water
1½ cups radishes, sliced
1 cup water chestnuts, sliced
1 bunch (about 6) green onions, sliced
2 pounds fresh bay shrimp, cooked
3 cups fried Chinese noodles, (crunchy type)
1 tablespoon fresh cilantro, minced
1 tablespoon sesame seeds

Dressing:

½ cup soy sauce
⅓ cup rice wine vinegar
3 tablespoons sugar
1 teaspoon dark sesame oil
1 clove garlic, minced
¼ teaspoon dried red pepper flakes

In a large bowl, mix together the Chinese egg noodles, bean sprouts, cucumber, broccoli, radishes, water chestnuts and green onions and set aside. Whisk together the dressing ingredients and pour over salad. Toss lightly and chill for 1 hour. Toss the salad occasionally to distribute the dressing. Right before serving, stir in the bay shrimp and fried Chinese crunchy noodles. Garnish with cilantro and sesame seeds.

Kathy Goans
Tualatin Vineyards

▪ PASTA SALAD À LA GRECQUE ▪

This Pasta Salad is a welcome treat and change from regular pasta salads. The Mediterranean flavor is the secret of its success.

2 cups rotini pasta, vegetable flavor or plain
1 head Romaine lettuce, torn into bite-sized pieces
2 ripe tomatoes, diced
1 red onion, quartered and thinly sliced
1 green pepper, diced
2 tablespoons fresh parsley, minced
½ pound Feta cheese, diced
½ cup pitted Greek olives, quartered
¼ cup olive oil
Juice of 1 lemon
1 teaspoon Greek oregano
Salt and pepper to taste

Cook rotini in boiling water until tender. Drain and cool.

Place Romaine, tomatoes, onion, green pepper and parsley in a large serving bowl. Toss well. Add rotini, Feta cheese and olives and toss again. Whisk together olive oil, lemon juice, Greek oregano, salt and pepper in a small bowl. Pour dressing over salad and toss to coat well. Serve with fresh bread.

Evangelia K. O'Dell

▪ JAPANESE CABBAGE SALAD ▪

1 head green cabbage, thinly sliced
2 cups cooked chicken, diced
1 bunch green onions, sliced
¼ cup blanched almonds, sliced

Dressing:

⅓ cup sugar
⅓ cup rice vinegar
½ cup vegetable oil

Crispy Chinese noodles

Combine cabbage, chicken, green onions and almonds in a large bowl.

For the dressing:

Dissolve the sugar in the vinegar. Whisk in the oil.

At least 1 hour before serving, toss the salad together with the dressing and chill.

Top with crispy noodles and serve.

Senator Bob Packwood

Snacks in Space

Imagine trying to eat without using your hands. Astronauts face this challenge when they go out for a EVA, or space walk. Wearing a bulky suit and a protective helmet, it is impossible for a space walking astronaut to bring their hands to their mouth. Space walks can be heavy exercise and astronauts need to replenish calories while going about their tasks. Thus space snacks are a must.

NASA provides EVA astronauts with snacks by mounting food inside their space suits. The snacks are mounted at mouth level so that by craning forward, a hungry astronaut can grab a snack using their teeth and satisfy their appetite. In the same way, drinking water is provided through a tube inside the space helmet. Imagine enjoying a space snack while floating 200 miles above the Earth!

During Project Gemini in the 1960s, an astronaut brought an unauthorized snack on a mission by sneaking a sandwich in his space suit. NASA was not amused!

Rob Grover

What Ever Happened to the Transparent Woman?

Funded by the E. C. Brown Foundation, the exhibit was built in Cologne, Germany, and arrived at OMSI amid much fanfare in the local press. At one time she had her own theater on the museum's lower level. Several years ago, the automated theater show became an interactive display; now the Transparent Woman has become part of the Whole Body exhibit at the new museum.

▪ RICHARD'S BLACK BEAN SALAD ▪

Great tasting high-fiber salad to complement chillable red wines, especially those like Amity Gamay Noir and Amity Nouveau Style Pinot Noir.

1½ cups cooked black beans
1 small green bell pepper, cut into bite-sized strips
1 small carrot, coarsely shredded
2 tablespoons red onion, finely chopped
2 tablespoons olive oil
2 tablespoons lime juice
¼ teaspoon lime zest, minced
⅛ teaspoon cumin
⅛ teaspoon cayenne
Lettuce leaves, sliced lime, strawberries or beet slices for garnish

In a bowl, combine cooked black beans, green pepper, carrot and onion. In a small, covered jar combine olive oil, lime juice and zest, cumin and cayenne. Cover, shake well and pour over bean mixture. Toss well and chill thoroughly. Stir before serving on a bed of lettuce. Garnish with lime slices, strawberries and beet slices.

Vikki Wetle
Amity Vineyards

▪ JANET'S SALAD ▪

This recipe gets many requests.

1 head broccoli, chopped
1 head cauliflower, chopped
1½ cups celery, chopped
1 16-ounce package frozen tiny peas, thawed and drained
1 pound bacon; cooked, drained and crumbled

Dressing:

2 cups mayonnaise
¼ cup onion, chopped
¼ cup fresh Parmesan cheese, grated
¼ cup sugar
2 tablespoons vinegar
1¼ teaspoons salt

Combine salad ingredients in a large serving bowl and chill. Blend dressing ingredients in a blender or food processor until smooth. Pour over salad and toss. Serves 8 to 10.

Mary Bence

▪ ANTIPASTA PASTA SALAD ▪

Dressing:

3 cloves garlic, minced
½ cup Balsamic vinegar
2 teaspoons dried basil, crushed in a mortar and pestle
2 teaspoons dried oregano, crushed in a mortar and pestle
1 teaspoon dried rosemary, crushed in a mortar and pestle
1 teaspoon salt
½ teaspoon dried hot red pepper flakes
¾ cup olive oil

Pasta Salad:

1 pound rotini pasta, cooked and drained
1½ cups salami, cut into ¼-inch dice
1½ cups mozzarella, cut into ¼-inch dice
1½ cups Kalamata olives, pitted and cut into ¼-inch dice
1 cup marinated artichoke hearts, drained and cut into ¼-inch dice
1 cup pepperecinis, seeded and cut into ¼-inch dice
3 cups broccoli, cauliflower or carrots cut into 1-inch pieces, blanched in boiling water for about 1 minute or until barely tender, then refreshed in ice water

Combine dressing ingredients and set aside. Place the cooked, hot pasta in a large bowl and toss with the dressing. Combine remaining ingredients and toss with the pasta and dressing. Allow to marinate, refrigerated, overnight before serving.

Leslie J. Whipple

Meteor Showers

Quadrantids: January 3; Fair view; 80 meteors per hour.

Lyrids: April 22; Excellent view; 15 meteors per hour.

Aquarids: May 5; Poor view; 60 meteors per hour.

Perseids: August 12; Excellent view; 95 meteors per hour.

Orinids: October 21; Good view; 30 meteors per hour.

Taurids: November 3; Fair view; 15 meteors per hour.

Leonids: November 17; Very good View; 15 meteors per hour.

Geminids: December 13; Excellent view; 90 meteors per hour.

▪ GERMAN POTATO SALAD ▪

This recipe makes a large bowl of potato salad, so divide recipe in half for a smaller amount.

12 potatoes; boiled in their jackets until just tender, then peeled and sliced
12 hard-cooked eggs, peeled and chopped
1 pound bacon; cooked until crisp then crumbled, reserve ½ cup bacon drippings
6 large dill pickles, finely diced
1 small onion, finely diced
½ cup reserved bacon drippings
2 raw eggs, very fresh
1½ to 2 cups mayonnaise
1 tablespoon dill pickle juice
1 tablespoon vinegar
1 teaspoon salt
1 teaspoon pepper

In a very large bowl, combine potatoes, hard-cooked eggs, crumbled bacon, pickles and onion. Gently toss together. In a separate bowl, beat together the cooled bacon drippings and raw eggs. Add mayonnaise, pickle juice, vinegar, salt and pepper and beat until smooth. Pour this dressing over the potato mixture and toss to coat well. Refrigerate for at least 3 hours before serving. Store in the refrigerator.

Martha and Michael White

▪ PARMESAN SALAD DRESSING ▪

1 cup vegetable oil
½ cup fresh Parmesan cheese, grated
¼ cup white wine vinegar
1 to 2 cloves garlic, minced
½ teaspoon black pepper
¼ teaspoon cloves

Place all ingredients in a blender or food processor and blend until smooth. Chill before using. Makes 1¾ cups of dressing.

Lisa Lemco

▪ CAESAR SALAD ▪

1 large head Romaine lettuce; washed, dried and torn into bite-sized pieces
1½ cups fresh Parmesan cheese, grated
1 2-ounce can flat anchovies, minced
Juice of 1 lemon
1 large clove garlic, minced
1 teaspoon Dijon mustard
1 teaspoon red wine vinegar
½ cup olive oil

Place Romaine, Parmesan and anchovies in a large salad bowl. Combine lemon juice and garlic in a small bowl and allow to stand for 10 minutes. Add mustard and vinegar and blend well. Whisk in olive oil and pour over salad. Toss well to distribute all ingredients.

Stewart M. Whipple

▪ BLUE CHEESE DRESSING ▪

1¼ cups blue cheese, crumbled
1 cup mayonnaise
1 cup sour cream
¾ cup buttermilk
2 teaspoons prepared horseradish
1 teaspoon dry mustard
1 teaspoon garlic, minced
1 teaspoon vinegar
½ teaspoon salt
½ teaspoon white pepper

In a large bowl, combine all ingredients and blend until smooth. Cover and chill for at least 3 hours before serving to allow the flavors to marry. Makes about 2 pints.

Charles W. Manke

▪ CHEF'S DRESSING ▪

1 large egg, very fresh
1 tablespoon prepared mustard
2 teaspoons salt
¼ teaspoon garlic, minced
6 tablespoons cider vinegar
2 tablespoons tarragon-flavored white wine vinegar
2 cups vegetable oil
½ cup water

Put egg, mustard, salt and garlic in a blender and blend on medium speed for 30 seconds. Add vinegars and blend an additional 10 seconds. Increase speed to high, and with blender running, add the oil in a thin, steady stream. Then add water in a thin, steady stream. The dressing should be very smooth, creamy and thick. Use immediately.

Donna L. Kaseberg

Meteor showers occur when swarms of orbiting particles left by comets blast into the atmosphere at 135,000 mph. They collide with gas atoms and molecules, and become wrapped in a glowing sheath of heated air and vaporized material boiled off their surfaces.

Most of these things are chunks of dust that range in size from a grain of sand on up to the size of a lima bean. Before entering the atmosphere, a fragment is called a "meteoroid." The flash of light 60 to 70 miles high in the Earth's atmosphere is called a "meteor," and any piece of a meteoroid that survives the fiery plunge and reaches the Earth is a "meteorite."

Bruce Spainhower

SOUPS

▪ The Murdock Sky Theater ▪

The sunset was over in the blink of an eye. The stars appeared only seconds later. The whole sky whirled overhead as time advanced at an unnatural pace. Suddenly, the familiar stars gave way to galaxies pin-wheeling overhead, which in turn vanished in a burst of laser light. We found ourselves transported to an eerie alien landscape with strange mountains rimming the horizon.

Was it all a dream? No, just a few minutes out of an average afternoon in OMSI's *Murdock Sky Theater*. It's a unique place where technology puts a face on science, where the complex concepts of astronomy become a little more friendly. And while it's not all done with mirrors, the magic behind the scenes has a story all its own.

Overhead is the giant domed projection screen spanning just over 52 feet. Underneath, reclined seats for 200 encircle the spacecraft-like star projector on a gently sloping floor. Around the periphery, an odd collection of lenses point skyward from various pieces of equipment. In one part of the room is a control center, with lights, knobs, computers, and even more unidentifiable equipment. With this combination, the *Sky Theater* planetarium creates the effective illusion of the night sky with a few added features mother nature never intended.

Unlike a movie theater where a single projector does the job, a planetarium is a "multi-media" theater with dozens of projectors working in concert to create the show. Most of them are modified slide projectors, with miniature mechanisms inside to create the animations seen on the dome. Even the star projector is nothing more than a collection of some 50 individual slide projectors plus an amazing set of motors and gears to impart motion to the sky.

Behind the low wall surrounding the room sits the massive laser projector with its 3.5 watt water-cooled laser and a set of electronically controlled optics as complex as the rest of the theater. And suspended twenty feet above the floor behind the dome are the speakers from the four-channel theater sound system.

Each time a show runs, all of the theater components perform on cue, orchestrated by the commands of a central control computer. While this may seem complicated, a "building-block" approach to planetarium shows affords a tremendous amount of flexibility. Feature shows can incorporate the latest discoveries. Laser light shows always have a new look; and shows for schools can adapt "on the fly" to the needs of the group.

So no matter when you visit the *Sky Theater*, you'll be guaranteed a unique experience, a chance to catch a glimpse of a new corner of the universe. And you'll be there and back in under an hour.

Bruce Spainhower
Theater Operations Manager

▪ MEATLESS BLACK BEAN SOUP ▪

2¼ cups dried black beans, rinsed in a colander
10 cups water
1 tablespoon vegetable oil
2 large onions, chopped
2 stalks celery **OR** 1 small green pepper, chopped
2 cloves garlic, minced
3 to 4 tablespoons dried cilantro **OR** ⅓ cup fresh cilantro, minced
2½ teaspoons chili powder
¾ teaspoon black pepper
½ teaspoon Tabasco sauce, or to taste
¼ teaspoon allspice
2 beef bouillon cubes
3 tablespoons lemon juice
1 8-ounce can tomato sauce
1 15-ounce can Mexican-style stewed tomatoes
Salt to taste
Plain yogurt

Place beans in a large pot, cover with 10 cups water and soak overnight. Do not drain.

Heat oil in a large skillet. Add onions and sauté until translucent. Add sautéed onions, celery or green pepper, garlic, cilantro, chili powder, pepper, Tabasco, allspice and bouillon cubes to beans and water. Bring to a boil, then reduce heat to low and simmer, covered, for 2 to 3 hours, or until beans are very tender.

Stir in lemon juice, tomato sauce and Mexican-style tomatoes. Partially mash beans with a potato masher. Season with salt to taste. Return soup to a simmer and cook about 15 minutes. Serve with a dollop of yogurt in each bowl of soup. Serves about 6.

Janet Filips

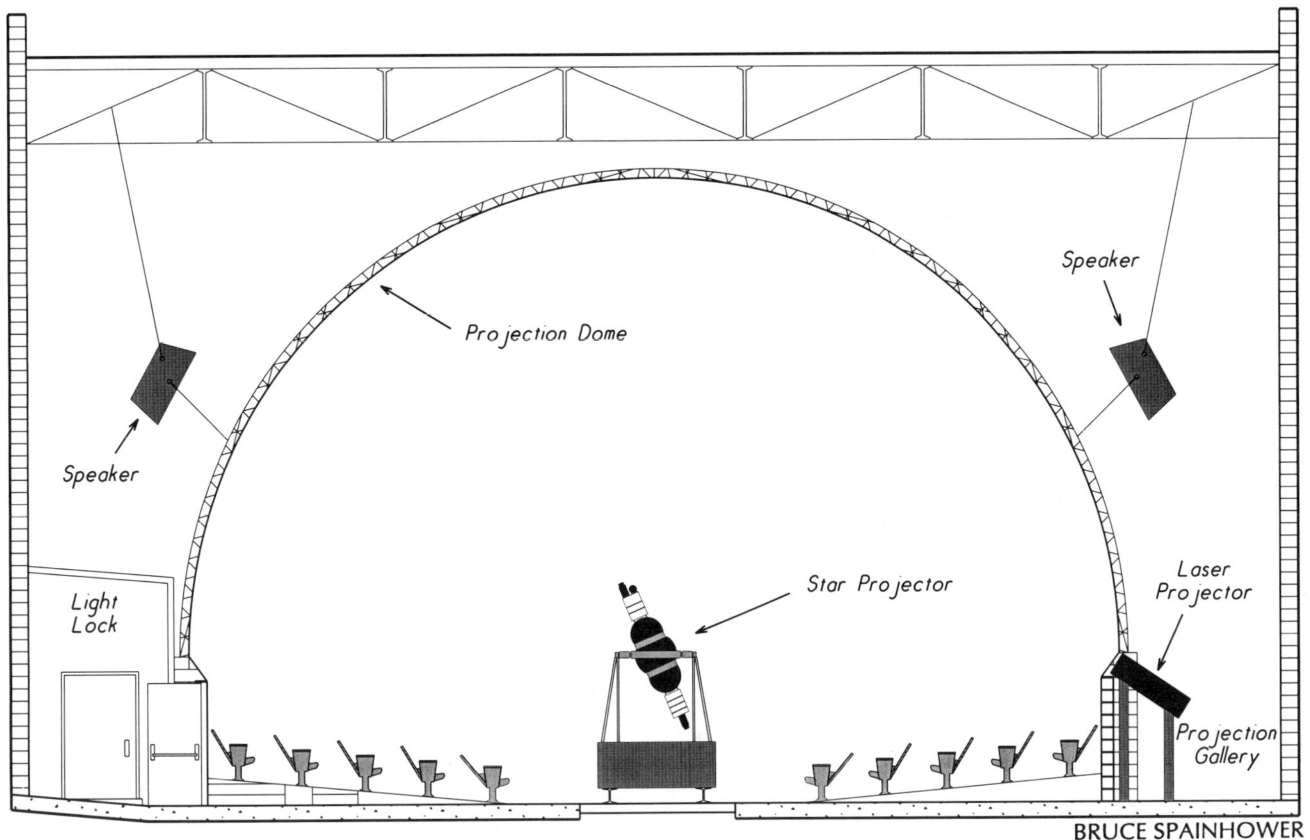

BRUCE SPAINHOWER

▪ RIBOLLITA ▪

I first tasted Ribollita (which means boiled again) at Lorenza de' Medici's Badia a Coltibuono. My mentor, Paola Ceccarilli, taught me how to perfect this hearty Tucsan Soup.

⅓ cup olive oil
1 slice pancetta, diced
2 cloves garlic, minced
1 small onion, peeled and chopped
2 carrots, peeled and sliced
½ cup cabbage, chopped
1 stalk celery, chopped
2 tablespoons Italian parsley, minced
1 potato, peeled and diced
1 beet, peeled and diced
2 cups tomatoes and their juice
2 quarts chicken stock
Salt and pepper to taste
1 15-ounce can cannelini beans
5 thick slices firm Italian bread, cut into 1-inch cubes
Parmesan cheese, grated

Heat olive oil in a large, heavy pot over medium heat. Add pancetta and sauté until crisp. Add garlic and sauté just until fragrant. Add onion, carrots, cabbage and celery and parsley and sauté until golden. Add potato, beet, tomatoes and stock. Season with salt and pepper. Bring to a boil, then reduce heat to low and simmer until vegetables are tender, about 45 minutes. Stir in beans and heat through. Remove soup from heat and allow to cool. Cover and refrigerate overnight.

The next day, add bread to soup, making sure that bread is covered by the soup. Bring to a boil, then reduce heat to low and simmer until all of the bread has been absorbed into the soup, about 45 minutes. Ladle soup into bowls and serve with Parmesan cheese sprinkled on top.

Patricia Wied

Primordial Soup

There are a variety of theories associated with the origins of life on Earth. One theory that has actually had some experimental evidence to support it is the "Primordial Soup" theory. It helps explain how living organisms might have emerged in a rather hostile, cooling planet environment.

CH_4 Methane
NH_3 Ammonia
H_2 Hydrogen
H_2O Water
(All early atmospheric gasses)

Mix all ingredients in a shallow, tide-pool like crevasse. Strike with lightening. Check for complex organic molecules in resulting residue. Let residue sit for thousands of years. Keep striking with lightning and/or heating with volcanic reactions. Check again, this time for simple microbe life forms.

David Heil
Newton's Apple
Associate Director, OMSI

▪ SHRIMP BISQUE ▪

1 tablespoon butter
1 tablespoon fresh ginger, minced
2 to 3 cloves garlic, minced
2 cups mushrooms, thinly sliced
1 pound small shrimp
4 cups cream
½ cup tomato sauce
3 tablespoons teriyaki sauce, (I use "Sagawa's" brand)
¼ teaspoon cayenne pepper
Fresh cilantro for garnish

In a large saucepan, melt the butter over medium heat. Stir in the ginger and garlic and sauté until just fragrant. Add the mushrooms and sauté until tender. Add shrimp, cream, tomato sauce, teriyaki sauce and cayenne pepper. Reduce heat to low and simmer for about 30 minutes. Serve with a little chopped cilantro on top. Serves 6.

Sanji Elliot

▪ BARBARA SUE SEAL'S COMFORT CHICKEN SOUP ▪

1 Oregon-grown frying chicken, cut-up
2 cups celery with tops, chopped
1 cup tomato, chopped
2 carrots, chopped
1 large onion, sliced
1 bay leaf
1 teaspoon salt
½ teaspoon garlic powder
½ teaspoon pepper
2 cups noodles, uncooked
2 eggs, scrambled

In a large stock pot, put chicken, celery, tomato, carrots, onion, bay leaf, salt, garlic powder and pepper. Cover with cold water and bring to a boil. Reduce heat to low, cover and simmer for about 2 hours or until chicken is very tender and falls off the bone. Remove chicken and de-bone. Discard the bones. Return chicken meat to the pot. Stir in the noodles and scrambled eggs. Simmer uncovered until noodles are tender and serve. ENJOY!

Barbara Sue Seal
Barbara Sue Seal
Properties, Inc.

▪ SPANISH ALMOND SOUP ▪

3 tablespoons butter
1 large Spanish onion, finely chopped
6 cups chicken stock
¾ cup ground almonds
½ cup brown rice
2 hard-cooked eggs, chopped
½ teaspoon saffron threads
¼ teaspoon paprika
½ cup fresh parsley, minced

In a large pot, heat the butter over medium heat. Add onion and sauté until translucent. Stir in stock and bring to a boil. Reduce heat to low and simmer, covered, for 10 minutes. Add almonds, rice, eggs, saffron and paprika. Cover and simmer an additional 30 minutes. Stir in parsley and simmer, uncovered for 2 more minutes. Serves 6 to 8.

Leo and Olivia MacLeod

Stories being told to rapt listeners inside a 40-foot plastic whale.

▪ CREAM OF SWISS WHEAT SOUP ▪

This recipe was featured in Bon Appetit Magazine.

6 tablespoons butter
½ cup Quick Cream of Wheat
⅓ cup onion, minced
1 quart chicken stock
1 quart milk
Freshly ground white pepper to taste
Freshly ground nutmeg to taste
⅓ cup heavy cream
1 egg yolk
1 medium tomato; peeled, seeded and diced
Minced chives for garnish

Cook butter in a heavy saucepan over low heat until lightly browned. Stir in Cream of Wheat and cook until golden. Add onion and cook about 2 minutes. Add stock and milk, increase heat to medium-high and bring mixture to a boil, stirring constantly. Reduce heat to low and simmer 15 minutes, stirring often. Remove from heat and add pepper and nutmeg to taste. In a small bowl, whisk together cream and egg yolk. Blend cream mixture into soup. Stir in tomato. Serve immediately with a sprinkling of chives. Serves 8 to 10.

Kurt Mezger
Chalet Swiss Specialty Restaurant
Welches, Oregon

▪ HOT AND SOUR SOUP ▪

5 cups chicken stock
12 ounces firm tofu, diced
2 cups bean sprouts, coarsely chopped
4 to 6 mushrooms, sliced
1 8-ounce can water chestnuts, sliced
1 green onion, including green part, sliced
2 tablespoons white wine vinegar
1 tablespoon dry sherry
1 teaspoon soy sauce
½ teaspoon white pepper
¼ teaspoon Tabasco sauce
¼ cup cold water
2 tablespoons cornstarch
½ cup fresh or frozen peas
2 tablespoons egg substitute **OR** 1 egg, lightly beaten

Bring chicken stock to a boil in a large pot. Add tofu, bean sprouts, mushrooms, water chestnuts, green onion, vinegar, sherry, soy sauce, white pepper and Tabasco sauce and simmer for about 4 minutes. In a small bowl, stir together water and cornstarch until cornstarch is dissolved. Add to soup and cook for about 2 minutes. Add peas. Pour egg substitute into soup slowly, and simmer just until cooked. Serve immediately. Serves 6 to 8.

Beatrice Metzger

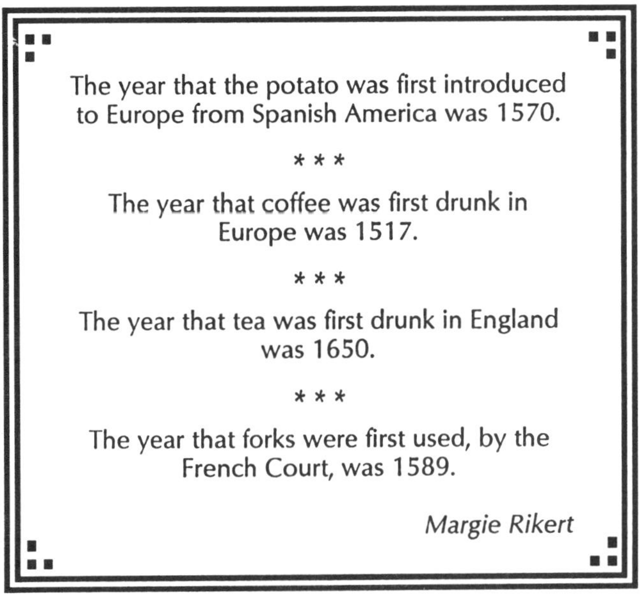

The year that the potato was first introduced to Europe from Spanish America was 1570.

* * *

The year that coffee was first drunk in Europe was 1517.

* * *

The year that tea was first drunk in England was 1650.

* * *

The year that forks were first used, by the French Court, was 1589.

Margie Rikert

▪ HARVEST WINE AND VEGETABLE SOUP ▪

This takes about 45 minutes for a wonderful homemade soup low in sodium and saturated fats. Serve with a young Oregon Pinot Noir or Nouveau-style Oregon Pinot Noir.

2 large Walla Walla onions **OR** yellow onions, chopped
3 carrots, peeled and diced
3 pink turnips **OR** parsnips **OR** yellow Finnish potatoes, peeled and diced
2 red bell peppers, diced
2 leeks (white part only), diced
2 tablespoons butter
1 tablespoon olive oil
2 cups Amity Nouveau **OR** Pinot Noir (plus 1 glass for the cook!)
1½ quarts chicken stock, low sodium
1 tablespoon arrowroot OR cornstarch
3 tablespoons cold water
2 tablespoons chives, minced
Salt and freshly ground pepper to taste
Croutons

Prepare all of the vegetables. In a large pot, melt the butter and olive oil over medium heat. Add vegetables and cook, stirring often, until barely soft. Add wine and simmer for 10 minutes, stirring often. Add the stock and bring to a simmer. Simmer 10 minutes, stirring occasionally. Dissolve arrowroot in cold water and stir into the soup. Simmer for about three minutes. Season with salt and pepper if desired. Serve garnished with chives and croutons. Serves 8.

Vikki Wetle
Amity Vineyards

▪ MYRON'S CRAB BUTTER SOUP ▪

This soup is a starter to a wonderful crab feast frequently enjoyed in the Amity household during the winter. This is a favorite of Myron Redford, owner and Winemaker of Amity Vineyards.

Crab butter from 2 or 3 Dungeness crabs, very fresh and uncleaned
½ cup milk **OR** cream
¼ cup dry sherry
¼ teaspoon curry powder

Tell your fish store that you want crabs that have good butter (the yellow matter that you usually throw away). Finish cleaning the crabs and refrigerate until ready to eat.

Gently combine crab butter and milk together in a heavy-bottomed saucepan. Bring to a simmer over low heat. Stir in sherry and curry powder and bring to a simmer. Remove from heat and serve immediately in warmed soup bowls. Serve with garlic bread and a crisp Oregon Chardonnay.

Myron Redford
Amity Vineyards

▪ BEEFY LENTIL SOUP ▪

1 pound ground chuck
1 pound bulk Italian sausage
1 cup dried lentils, rinsed
1 cup carrots, peeled and diced
1 cup celery, diced
1 cup onion, chopped
1 cup cabbage, chopped
1 teaspoon green pepper, minced
1 teaspoon salt
½ teaspoon pepper
1 bay leaf
2 beef bouillon cubes
1 46-ounce can tomato juice
4 cups water

In a large pot, brown beef and sausage over medium heat. Drain off fat. Stir in remaining ingredients and bring to a boil. Reduce heat to low and simmer, uncovered, for about 1½ hours or until lentils are very tender.

Dotti Wilson

What Ever Happened to the Walk-Through Heart?

One of the museum's most popular early exhibits, the heart allowed visitors to become part of the bloodstream and travel through this vital organ. After a stint inside the building, the heart was weatherized and outfitted with a slide to become a favorite playground activity for OMSI's youthful visitors. But it was never intended to be permanent, and eventually became too battered to remain.

▪ OLD WORLD SOUP ▪

This soup is from Austria and Hungary.

2 tablespoons bacon drippings
1½ pounds pork shoulder, cut into ½-inch cubes
2 medium onions, chopped
1 pound sauerkraut, drain and save juice
2 tablespoons flour
2 tablespoons brown sugar
2 tablespoons tomato paste
1 tablespoon paprika
4 beef bouillon cubes
4 cups water
Salt and pepper to taste
Sour cream

Heat bacon drippings in a large pot over medium heat. Add pork and onion and brown on all sides. Stir in drained sauerkraut. Add flour, brown sugar, tomato paste and paprika and stir until smooth. Cook for 15 minutes, stirring often. Add reserved sauerkraut juice, beef bouillon, water, salt and pepper to taste. Bring to a boil, then reduce heat to low. Cover and simmer for 45 to 50 minutes. Serve with a dollop of sour cream on top of each bowl. Serve 4 to 6.

Toni J. Ives

▪ WINTER VEGETABLE SOUP ▪

This is one of my favorite soups. I made it one winter day when I had too little of any one primary ingredient. We have been enjoying it ever since. I hope you will too.

4 tablespoons butter
1 medium onion, chopped
2 stalks celery, thinly sliced
1 small parsnip, peeled and chopped
1 carrot, peeled and chopped
1 small potato, peeled and chopped
¼ teaspoon thyme
4 to 8 cups chicken stock
Cream, optional
Salt and white pepper to taste

Heat the butter in a large pot over medium heat. Add the onion and sauté until tender and transparent. Add the celery and sauté until tender. Add parsnip, carrot, potato and thyme and enough stock to cover vegetables. Bring to a simmer, cover and reduce heat to low, and cook until vegetables are tender, about 15 to 20 minutes.

Puree soup in a blender in batches until it is very smooth. Put soup back in pot and add more stock if it needs thinning. You may also add some cream to make a richer soup. Season to taste with salt and white pepper. Heat through and serve.

Dennis Baker
Cafe des Amis
Portland, Oregon

▪ MAMA KINNEY'S PIZOLE ▪

3 tablespoons olive oil, or more
1 medium onion, chopped
2 cloves garlic, minced
¼ teaspoon dried red pepper flakes
1 pound lean pork, cut into ¾-inch cubes
Flour
8 cups chicken stock
¼ cup cilantro, minced
2 medium tomatoes, seeded and diced
1½ teaspoons oregano
Salt and pepper to taste
1 29-ounce can white hominy, drained and rinsed
Juice of 1 lime

Heat oil in a large pot over medium heat. Sauté onions for about 5 minutes or until just tender. Add garlic and red pepper and sauté for 2 to 3 minute or until fragrant; do not let garlic burn. Remove to a bowl and set aside.

Dredge pork cubes in flour and shake off the excess. Add to remaining oil in pot, adding more oil if necessary, and brown on all sides. Return onion mixture to pot. Stir in chicken stock, whisking up any browned bits in pot. Add cilantro, tomatoes, oregano, salt and pepper, hominy and lime juice. Bring to a boil then reduce heat to low. Simmer, partially covered, over low heat for about 45 minutes, or until pork and hominy are very tender.

Serve with French bread, bowls of chopped onion, cilantro and lime slices.

Leo MacLeod

▪ PAM'S CREAM OF LEEK AND BROCCOLI SOUP ▪

1 cup butter
1 medium leek, including the green part, finely sliced
1½ cups chopped broccoli
6 tablespoon flour
2 quarts milk, or more
1 teaspoon nutmeg
1 teaspoon salt
½ teaspoon black pepper

Melt butter in a pot over medium-low heat. Add leek and broccoli and sauté for 20 minutes. Whisk in flour until smooth. Add milk in a thin stream, whisking constantly until smooth. Add more milk if thinner soup is desired. Add nutmeg, salt and pepper. Reduce heat to low and simmer, stirring often, for about 45 minutes. Do not let soup boil. Serve with your favorite bread.

Bradley Cook

VEGETABLES

▪ The OMNIMAX Theater ▪

Early this century, motion picture theaters sprang up everywhere across the country. The "new" technology offered an experience without compare, a magic window that showed you the world for just a nickel. Oh, the images were a bit jumpy, the color was supplied by your imagination, and the sound was only as good as the local organist. But still, on any Saturday afternoon, you could walk down to the corner and escape into the Old West, the jungles of Africa, or the deserts of Egypt. People couldn't get enough of it.

But times changed, and what was once magic became ordinary. No longer satisfied with just a taste of realism, audiences wanted something different, something more. An evolution began that continues today. First came sound, somewhat scratchy and tinny, but at least when lips moved, words came out. Then came the miracle of color, a breathtaking dimension that made you feel like you could reach right through the screen and touch the world on the other side. Soon there were some remarkable variations—stereo sound, wide-screen, and even 3-D. But even with continual improvements, the formula for a movie theater remained pretty much the same. Yet people wanted even *more* realism.

The answer was as plain as a picture. Experienced photographers had long known that a larger film size gave a more realistic picture. But no one knew how to apply this to the movies, where the film has to move through the projector at the rate of twenty four pictures a second. Bigger film meant higher speeds, which almost always meant shredded film. Then everything changed in the early sixties. IMAX Corporation developed a breakthrough technology called the "Rolling Loop". The new system could easily move a frame of film ten times larger than standard movie film into and out of a projector at the speeds required. As each frame comes to a stop behind the lens, it is held in place by a vacuum with microscopic accuracy. The resulting image is far sharper, steadier, and clearer than in any standard theater. A new six-channel sound system matches the visual realism of the IMAX system. The view through this new window of technology is simply incredible.

With such a vast improvement in motion picture quality, what could be left? There was only one thing: to remove the window entirely. A variation called OMNIMAX expands the IMAX picture and wraps it around you. The traditional movie screen at the end of the room becomes a dome, towering five stories over and around you, filling your entire field of vision. The effect must be experienced to be appreciated. It no longer *feels* like a movie, it *feels* like the real thing.

So now you can walk down to the corner, (of OMSI) and escape into the jungles of Africa, the depths of the ocean, or to the edge of outer space. Each journey offers a realism unmatched by anything but the original experience. And while the price is no longer a nickel, the magic of a world seen through OMNIMAX is something you'll never forget.

Bruce Spainhower
Theater Operations Manager

▪ ARTICHOKE AND SPINACH CASSEROLE ▪

2 6-ounce jars marinated artichoke hearts; drain and reserve oil
3 10-ounce packages frozen chopped spinach, thawed and well-drained
6 eggs, lightly beaten
1½ cups sharp Cheddar cheese, grated
½ cup onion, chopped
1 2-ounce jar pimento, (optional)
1 or 2 cloves garlic, minced
½ teaspoon savory
¼ teaspoon salt
⅛ teaspoon black pepper

Preheat oven to 350 degrees. Oil 9-inch by 13-inch baking dish with reserved oil from marinated artichoke hearts.

Cut drained artichoke hearts into pieces and arrange in the bottom of prepared baking dish.

In a large bowl, combine spinach, eggs, 1¼ cups cheese, onion, pimento, garlic, savory, salt and pepper. Mix until well blended then spread over artichoke hearts in baking dish. Sprinkle with reserved cheese. Bake for 30 minutes, or until heated through and bubbly.

Corky Poppert

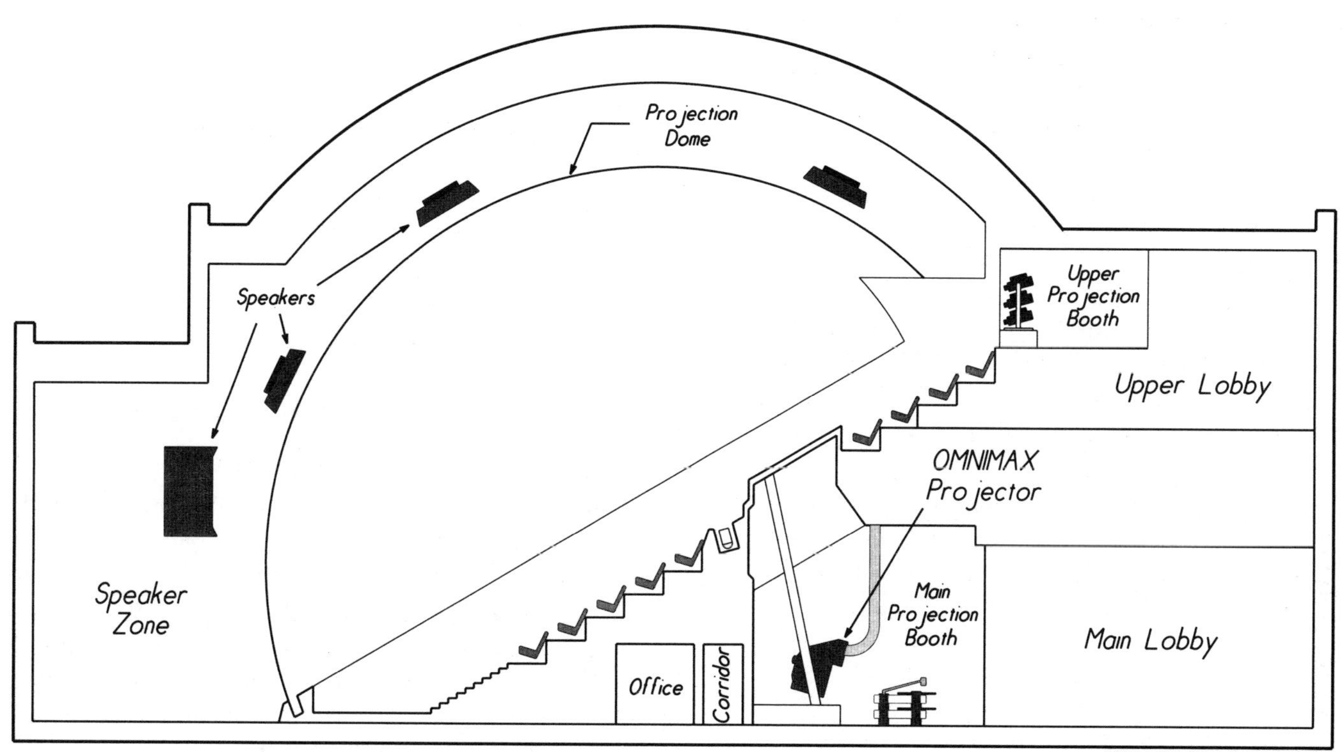

BRUCE SPAINHOWER

What Ever Happened to the Smoker's Lung?

A smoking and health exhibit in the 1970s featured human lungs from smokers and non-smokers, side by side. The lungs were attached to a respirator, so visitors could see how the pink, healthy lung inflated to a larger size, and how the smoker's lung was slower to deflate. Due to the need to preserve it every night in an arsenic solution, the lung exhibit could not be consistently maintained.

▪ COWBOY BEANS ▪

- 2 pounds pinto beans, washed and picked over to remove any grit
- 12 cups cold water
- 2 pounds stew meat, diced
- 8 ounces salt pork, diced
- 2 cups onion, chopped
- 6 to 8 cloves garlic, minced
- 3 pickled hot peppers, minced
- 2 16-ounce cans tomato sauce
- 1 teaspoon oregano
- 1 teaspoon salt
- ½ teaspoon monosodium glutamate (optional)

The day before serving Cowboy Beans, place washed beans in a large stock pot and cover with 12 cups cold water. Bring to a boil, then reduce heat to low and simmer beans, covered, for 1½ hours. Remove from heat and let cool. Refrigerate overnight.

The next day, add remaining ingredients and bring to a boil. Reduce heat to low and simmer, uncovered, for about 4 hours, or until beans are very tender and mixture has thickened.

Corky Poppert

▪ LEEK CAKES ▪

- 4 cups leeks; white part only, chopped medium fine
- 1½ cups milk
- 2 eggs, beaten
- 1 cup flour
- ½ teaspoon baking powder
- ¼ teaspoon sugar
- Salt and pepper to taste
- Olive oil for frying

In a large bowl, mix milk and eggs until blended. Add flour, baking powder, sugar, salt and pepper and stir until smooth. Add chopped leeks and mix well. Heat about 2 tablespoons olive oil in a large skillet over medium heat. Place about ¼ cup of mixture per cake into skillet. Cook until nicely browned, then turn, and cook on other side until done. Continue until all leek mixture is used. Keep Leek Cakes warm in a 200 degree oven until all Cakes are done.

Ken and Dorothy Brace

▪ GERMAN POTATO PANCAKES ▪

- 6 potatoes, peeled and grated
- 2 small onions, peeled and grated
- 3 eggs
- 3 tablespoons flour
- ½ teaspoon salt
- Oil for cooking
- Maple syrup as an accompaniment

In a large mixing bowl, combine grated potatoes, grated onions, eggs, flour and salt. Mix well. Heat about 2 tablespoons oil in a skillet over medium heat. Place about ¼ cup of mixture per pancake into skillet. Cook until nicely browned, then turn, and cook on other side until done. Continue until all potato mixture is used. Keep pancakes warm in a 200 degree oven until all pancakes are done. Serve with maple syrup.

Blanche Zitzewitz

▪ MELENZANA ALLA PARMIGIANA ▪

EGGPLANT PARMESAN

1 1-pound 4-ounce can whole tomatoes
1 6-ounce can tomato paste
2 tablespoons olive oil
Salt and pepper to taste
2 cups bread crumbs
½ cup Parmesan cheese, grated
1 tablespoon fresh parsley, minced
2 cloves garlic, minced
1 large eggplant
6 tablespoons olive oil
½ pound Mozzarella cheese, thinly sliced

Preheat oven to 375 degrees. Lightly grease a 9-inch by 13-inch baking dish.

In a large sauce pan, combine tomatoes, tomato paste, 2 tablespoons olive oil and ¼ teaspoon salt. Stir until well blended. Simmer, uncovered, over low heat for 30 minutes, stirring occasionally.

In a medium bowl, mix together bread crumbs, Parmesan cheese, parsley, garlic and a little salt and pepper to taste. Set aside.

Wash, dry and slice eggplant crosswise into ½-inch slices. Place eggplant slices in a bowl, cover with hot water and let stand for 5 minutes. Drain and dry eggplant slices well. Heat 6 tablespoons olive oil in a large skillet over medium heat. Sauté eggplant for about 3 minutes on each side, or until tender and lightly browned. Season with salt and pepper to taste and remove from pan.

Place a layer of eggplant in the bottom of prepared baking dish. Sprinkle with a layer of the bread crumb mixture. Pour a layer of tomato sauce over the bread crumbs. Alternate layers until all ingredients are used. Top with Mozzarella cheese. Bake for about 15 minutes, or until heated through and Mozzarella is lightly browned. Serve very hot. Serves 4 to 6.

Peter DeFazio
Member of Congress

▪ SWEET AND SOUR CARROTS ▪

2 pounds carrots, peeled and sliced
1 12-ounce can pureed tomatoes
1 medium onion, chopped
1 green pepper, seeded and chopped
½ cup sugar
¼ cup vinegar

Steam or boil carrots until just tender. Place carrots in a non-reactive bowl, such as glass, ceramic or stainless steel. Combine remaining ingredients in a sauce pan and bring to a boil. Boil for about 1 minute, or until sugar is dissolved, whisking constantly. Pour sauce over carrots and stir gently to coat completely. Marinate at least 1 hour or more. Reheat or serve cold.

Barbara Curtis

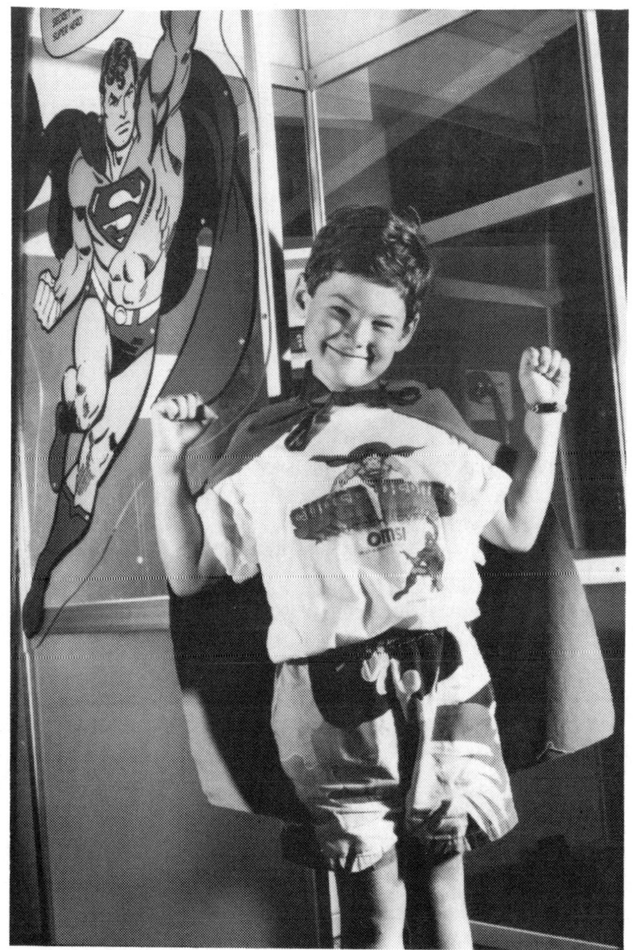

▪ EGGPLANT AND TOMATO STACKS ▪

½ cup olive oil
1 clove garlic, minced
2 teaspoons Italian seasoning
1 teaspoon salt
1 teaspoon sugar
1 large eggplant, peeled and cut into 12 slices
4 medium tomatoes, cut into 3 thick slices
¼ cup Parmesan cheese, grated

In a small bowl, whisk together olive oil, garlic, Italian seasoning, salt and sugar. Place eggplant slices in a single layer on the rack of a broiler pan. Brush with olive oil mixture and broil 6-inches from heat for 5 minutes. Turn and brush other side with olive oil mixture. Broil 5 minutes. Top with tomato slices, brush with olive oil mixture and sprinkle with Parmesan. Broil an additional 2 minutes or until heated through and cheese is golden brown.

Dotti Wilson

Buttered Asparagus

Start with 1-pound of fresh asparagus. Wash thoroughly and remove the scales along the stem. Tie the stalks into bunches with string. Place upright in a narrow, deep pan standing in 1-inch of salt water (the asparagus, not you). Cover and boil for 10 to 15 minutes, until tender/crisp. Use a fork to catch the string to lift asparagus out whole. Season with salt, pepper, (I prefer garlic salt) or spice of your choosing (I discourage cinnamon). Pour melted butter on top.

If you choose to use a low-fat substitute instead of butter, then change the name of the recipe to Low Fat Substituted Asparagus.

Stephen M. Anderson

The Babe and I

CRACK!!! Another homer over the left field fence. Babe Ruth pudgely pounces around the base path. "Wow!" I thought to myself as I contemplated the amazing similarities between the Babe and me.

Despite many years at bat, I have never put one out of the park. I have never pitched a single inning. My batting average was average at best. But the Babe and I share a contempt for asparagus. The amazing similarities do not end there. We both avoid asparagus for the same reason.

At a posh dinner party, the home run king pushed a platter of asparagus from his plate. The elegance of the party demanded a delicate response, "Asparagus makes my urine smell funny." The Babe was not known for his social graces.

I was shocked, maybe not as much as the dinner guests, and certainly not for the same reason. I thought everyone knew of the odiferous effects of the despised asparagus. As it turns out, the Babe and I share an uncommon pair of genetic predispositions.

The chemicals that cause the stench are S-methylthioacylate and S-methyl 3-(methylthio)thiopropionate. These sulfur containing compounds are related to mercaptans, the active ingredient in rotting vegetation. Only people with the proper gene produce the aroma as the digestive by-product of asparagus. A University of Birmingham study concurred with previous experiments that found 40 percent of us produce "asparagus urine." A lucky 6 percent produce a prominent pungency.

Some people may reek without knowing it. A study at the Hebrew University in Jerusalem found that a few people can not detect the odor at all. Most could detect "something funny" but only at high concentrations. A select 10 percent were hyper-sensitive to the smell and could detect trace amounts.

It is a rare bird indeed who not only produces the foul odor but can also detect it.

If you would like to do a little genetic testing, try the Buttered Asparagus recipe. Please excuse me if I politely decline a portion at your next dinner party. I am actually paying homage to my favorite baseball hero Babe Ruth.

Stephen M. Anderson

Just how strong is the acid in our stomachs?

Our stomachs secrete hydrochloric acid strong enough to dissolve metal. The stomach protects itself with a lining that contains base chemicals which neutralize the acid.

David Heil
Newton's Apple
Associate Director, OMSI

▪ FRESNO POTATO CASSEROLE ▪

2½ to 3 pounds medium potatoes
Water
4 slices bacon, crisply fried and crumbled
4 green onions, including the green part, sliced
1 cup sour cream
½ cup milk
1 cup Cheddar cheese, shredded
Salt and pepper to taste
¾ cup seasoned croutons, slightly crushed
3 tablespoons melted butter

Preheat oven to 350 degrees. Grease a 2-quart baking dish.

Place potatoes in a large pot and cover with water. Bring to a boil, over medium heat, and cook, partially covered, until potatoes are just tender, about 15 to 20 minutes. Drain well. When cool enough to handle, peel and cut into ¼-inch slices.

Arrange half the potatoes in prepared baking dish. Top with half of the bacon and green onion. Stir sour cream and milk together until smooth and spread half of the mixture over the bacon and green onions. Sprinkle half the cheese over the sour cream mixture. Season with salt and pepper. Repeat with remaining potato slices, bacon, green onion, sour cream mixture and cheese. Sprinkle with croutons and drizzle melted butter over the top.

Bake for about 30 minutes, or until hot and bubbly. Serves 6.

Lynda Johnston

▪ EGGPLANT MARILYNNE ▪

1 large eggplant
2 tablespoons butter
1 zucchini, diced
3 stalks celery, chopped
1 small onion, chopped
10 mushrooms, quartered
1 tomato, chopped
½ cup walnuts, chopped
1 teaspoon oregano
½ teaspoon basil
¼ teaspoon salt
Pepper to taste
8-ounces Mozzarella, grated

Preheat oven to 350 degrees. Lightly oil a 9-inch by 13-inch baking pan.

Cut eggplant in half length-wise. Scoop out the flesh, without damaging the shells, and cut flesh into ½-inch cubes. Place eggplant shells cut-side down in prepared pan and bake for 15 minutes. Remove from oven and turn cut-side up.

Heat butter in a large skillet over medium heat. Add cubed eggplant, zucchini, celery, onion, mushrooms, tomato, walnuts, oregano, basil, salt and pepper and sauté until just tender. Place mixture in eggplant shells and sprinkle with Mozzarella cheese. Return to oven and bake an additional 15 minutes or until tender.

Marilynne Eichinger

▪ SOUTHERN FRIED CABBAGE ▪

My father was born and raised in the Eastern Kentucky hills. I grew up on a diet of spicy, hillbilly cooking, heavy on cayenne, garlic and lots of bacon grease. The fact that I have extremely low cholesterol amazes me. This recipe is one of the family favorites handed down from my father. He never used a cookbook. With the hill people medicine, stories, songs and recipes were just "something you knew". I've modified the recipe over the years to decrease the amount of fat that was originally used.

3 to 5 thick slices bacon, diced
1 large head green cabbage, thickly sliced
1 28-ounce can whole tomatoes
½ teaspoon dill seed
1 small whole dried red cayenne pepper
¼ teaspoon freshly ground black pepper

In a large skillet, preferably cast iron, fry bacon over medium heat until almost crisp. Remove bacon from skillet and set aside. Pour off all but 1 or 2 tablespoons of bacon grease. Return skillet to heat. Add cabbage to pan and stir quickly to coat cabbage with bacon drippings. Reduce heat to low and add tomatoes and their liquid. Gradually increase heat to medium-high, being careful to avoid splatters. Stir cabbage briskly until it begins to wilt. Reduce heat to medium-low and add reserved bacon, dill seed, whole red pepper and black pepper. For very spicy cabbage crumble red pepper completely; for milder cabbage, crumble half the red pepper; for very mild cabbage leave the red pepper whole. Allow mixture to come to a simmer then reduce heat to low, cover and simmer for 40 minutes or until tender.

This dish is usually served as a side dish to a southern boiled dinner of hamhocks and green beans, cornbread, Virginia ham and curly endive salad.

Marcia Hale

▪ RANCH-STYLE LIMAS ▪

2 10-ounce packages frozen lima beans
1 1-pound 12-ounce can tomatoes
½ cup onion, chopped
¼ cup brown sugar
1 teaspoon chili powder
1 teaspoon salt
½ teaspoon garlic powder
¼ teaspoon cayenne
⅛ teaspoon black pepper
6 slices bacon, cut in half

Preheat oven to 350 degrees.

Combine lima beans, tomatoes, onion, brown sugar, chili powder, salt, cayenne and black pepper in a bean pot, or other oven-proof heavy pot, and mix well. Top with bacon slices. Cover and bake for 3 hours. Serves 6.

Dotti Wilson

Some Edible Flowers

Holly Hock
Nasturtium
Borage
Fuschia
Snap Dragon
Day Lilly
Annual Bachelor Button
Johnny Jump-up
Gem Marigold
Gladiola
Rose

*Organiculture
Portland,
Oregon*

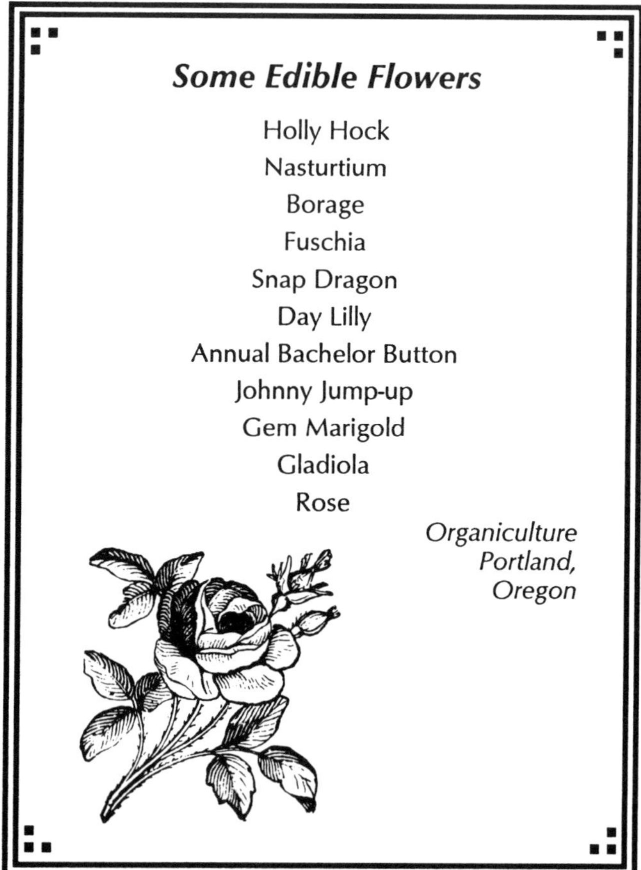

▪ SPINACH CASSEROLE ▪

3 10-ounce packages frozen chopped spinach; thawed and drained
8 ounces cream cheese
6 ounces Monterey Jack cheese, shredded
¼ cup melted butter
4 eggs, beaten
½ teaspoon salt
1 clove garlic, minced

Preheat oven to 350 degrees. Grease a 9-inch by 13-inch baking dish.

Squeeze as much moisture from spinach as possible. In a large bowl, combine all ingredients and mix well. Spread in prepared pan. Bake for about 30 to 40 minutes, or until hot and bubbly.

Tom Wenrick

▪ SUPER GLAZED CARROTS ▪

2 tablespoons butter
2 tablespoons minced onion
2 tablespoons minced parsley
8 medium carrots, peeled and cut into 1-inch pieces
1 14-ounce can beef consommé
⅛ teaspoon nutmeg

Heat butter in a medium sauce pan over medium heat. Add onion and parsley and sauté until onion is translucent. Add carrots, consommé and nutmeg. Cover and cook for 25 minutes. Uncover and cook an additional 20 minutes, or until carrots are tender and sauce has thickened and formed a glaze. Serves 4 to 6.

Toni J. Ives

▪ MAMA PORETTA'S EGGPLANT PARMESAN ▪

½ cup olive oil
2 medium onions, chopped
5 large cloves garlic, minced
2 tablespoons fennel seed
1 tablespoon fresh basil, minced
1 teaspoon oregano
1 # 10 can (1 gallon) stewed tomatoes
3 medium eggplants
1 cup milk
4 eggs, beaten
Italian seasoned bread crumbs
Oil for frying
2 cups Mozzarella cheese
1 cup Parmesan cheese

Preheat oven to 325 degrees. Lightly grease 2 9-inch by 13-inch baking pans.

Heat olive oil over medium heat in a large pot. Add onions, garlic, fennel, basil and oregano and sauté until onions are golden. Add tomatoes and bring to a boil. Reduce heat to low and simmer, uncovered, for 2 hours.

Peel the eggplant and cut into slices about ½-inch thick. Combine milk and eggs in a shallow dish. Place bread crumbs in a shallow dish. Dip eggplant in milk-egg mixture then in bread crumbs. Heat oil to 375 degrees. Put coated eggplant in deep-fryer and cook until brown and very tender. Remove eggplant and drain on paper towels.

Ladle about 4-ounces of tomato sauce into the bottom of prepared pan. Layer eggplant slices, some Mozzarella and Parmesan. Repeat until dish is full, ending with the two cheeses on top. Cover with foil and bake for 45 minutes.

Paul Lamberti

PASTA

▪ A BRIEF HISTORY OF LUNCHTIME ▪

Two Decades of Food at OMSI

From food vending machines to food service to our own full service Cafe—the OMSI restaurant has come a long way. Beginning in the old OMSI building, in the basement, over two decades ago, snack and drink machines stood around the sides of the wall where the Foucault pendulum swung. (Remember those red plastic pegs edging the circle?) A microwave was available later for the luxury of hot food. A short time after, a snack bar was added, with salads and sandwiches, run by one employee from a commercial food service. Somebody remembers the catchy name "Starlight Cafe" being given to the counter.

Then in 1988, a move was made to the old education section, with a huge increase in seating capacity to a staggering 42 people. Bolted wooden benches filled the second floor area which had a lovely three-way view of the park, the zoo and Canyon Road. Restaurant employees cursed the two story arrangement as supplies and garbage sacks had to be hand-carried in both directions.

Our splendid new facility owes a great deal to manager Paul Lamberti, who took over management in January 1990. All profits from the Cafe are returned to OMSI to help offset costs in other departments. We are proud of the handsome river-level dining area and patio with splendid views of the downtown skyline and a seating capacity of 382. We not only take care of food needs of the museum customer, the restaurant also caters for many in-house needs. It's a great place to work, we employees say, as we use real restaurant equipment and walk out the back door with the garbage dumpster mere steps away, and not a single stair among them.

Helen Hiatt

▪ PRAWN FETTUCINI ▪

This is a low cholesterol dish, no guilt!

1 pound prawns, shelled and deveined
½ cup olive oil
1 medium red onion, chopped
3 to 4 cloves garlic, minced
1 14-ounce can artichoke hearts in water, drained and chopped
4 to 5 medium tomatoes; peeled, seeded and chopped
12 ounces fettucini
Salt and pepper to taste

Poach the prawns in just enough simmering water to cover. Drain and set aside. Heat olive oil in a large skillet over medium-high heat. When hot, add onion and sauté for about 1 minute. Add garlic and sauté until fragrant. Add artichoke hearts and tomatoes and cook for about 2 minutes. Cook the fettucini according to package directions. Drain and stir into tomato mixture. Stir in prawns. Season with salt and pepper and serve immediately. Serves 4.

David H. Louis
Huber's Restaurant
Portland, Oregon

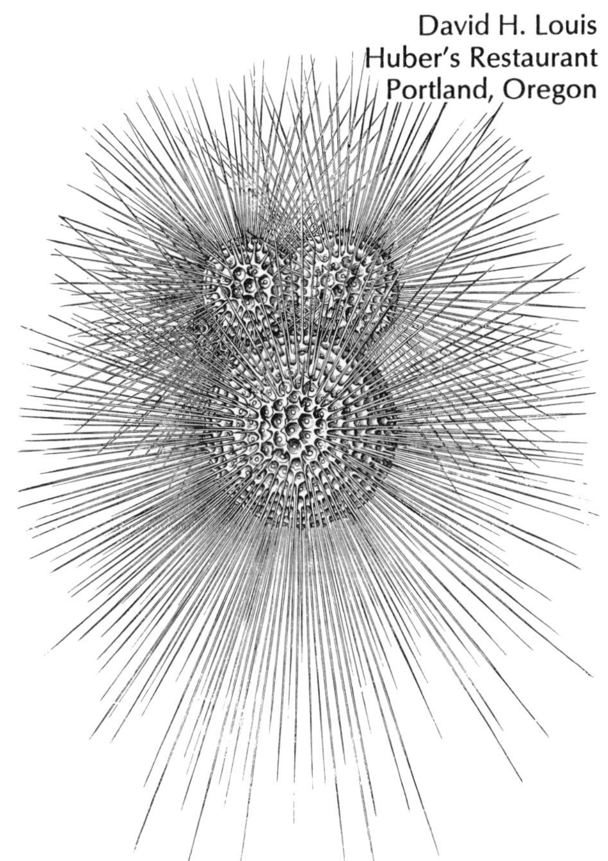

What Ever Happened to the Chick Hatchery and Humpty-Dumpty?

Up until a few years ago, OMSI featured live animal exhibits as hands-on natural science aids. One favorite among the younger visitors was the chick-hatching exhibit, where kids could pick up a newly-hatched bird after watching it peck its way out of the shell. The Humpty-Dumpty incubator contained asbestos to protect him from the heating elements; it was eventually removed for that reason.

▪ MACARONI AND CHEESE ▪

3 tablespoons butter
2 tablespoons flour
1 teaspoon dry mustard
1 teaspoon salt
¼ teaspoon cayenne
¼ teaspoon black pepper
2 cups milk
½ cup cream
2 cups Cheddar cheese, shredded
12 ounces macaroni, cooked and drained

Preheat broiler. Lightly oil a 2-quart baking dish.

In a large pot, melt butter over medium-high heat. Whisk in flour, mustard, salt, cayenne and black pepper and cook, stirring constantly for 1 minute. Pour in milk and cream, whisking constantly, and just bring to a boil. Remove from heat and stir in 1½ cups cheese until melted. Stir in cooked and drained macaroni and transfer to prepared baking dish. Sprinkle remaining cheese on top. Broil about 5 minutes or until golden.

Jenny Heflin

▪ KATIE'S SPECIAL MARINARA SAUCE ▪

1 small eggplant, diced
⅓ cup olive oil
4 tablespoons butter
1 medium onion, chopped
1 large green bell pepper, seeded and chopped
⅓ cup fresh parsley, minced
1 tablespoon minced garlic
½ pound sweet Italian sausage
2 28-ounce cans plum tomatoes and their liquid
1½ teaspoons pepper
Salt to taste

Sprinkle salt liberally over diced eggplant and place in a colander in the sink for 1 hour to drain excess liquid from eggplant. Rinse lightly and pat dry. Heat olive oil and butter together in a large pot over medium heat and add eggplant, onion, green pepper, parsley and garlic. Sauté until tender. In a skillet, brown sausage over medium heat. Drain off fat and add sausage to pot. Add tomatoes, pepper and salt and simmer over low heat for about 1 hour. Serve over pasta.

Leo MacLeod

What Ever Happened to the Periscope?

Still poking out through the roof in OMSI's Education Resource Center, the periscope originated in the late 1950s as part of a ship's bridge exhibit funded by Dr. Sam Diack. After the exhibit was disassembled and the Science Store was installed in the same area, visitors and employees continued to peer out with the periscope, most often toward the elephants at the Zoo.

▪ FETTUCINI CON FUNGHI ▪

½ cup extra virgin olive oil
1 pound fresh morel mushrooms, sliced
4 cloves garlic, finely chopped
½ cup Italian parsley, finely chopped
2 tablespoons fresh lemon juice
1 pound fresh egg fettucini, cooked until al dente and drained
¼ cup fresh Parmesan cheese, grated

Heat oil in a large sauté pan over medium-high heat. Add morels and sauté for 5 to 7 minutes. Add garlic and parsley and sauté an additional 2 minutes. Stir in lemon juice and toss with cooked fettucini. Garnish with Parmesan and serve. Serves 4.

Catherine Whims
Genoa
Portland, Oregon

▪ TAGLIERINI E GAMBERI ▪

¾ pound large shrimp; shelled, deveined and cut in half lengthwise
½ cup extra virgin olive oil
¼ cup garlic, finely chopped
¼ cup parsley (and wild fennel, if available), finely chopped
1 teaspoon dried red pepper flakes
Salt and pepper to taste
⅓ cup toasted, finely ground bread crumbs
1 pound fresh Taglierini pasta (or other fresh pasta), cooked until al dente and drained

In a large sauté pan, heat olive oil over medium heat. Add garlic and sauté until a light gold color. Add parsley and red pepper. Increase heat to high and add shrimp, sauté until cooked through. Season with salt and pepper to taste. Toss with bread crumbs and hot pasta. Garnish with additional bread crumbs and serve. Serves 4.

Catherine Whims
Genoa
Portland, Oregon

▪ WHITE LASAGNA ▪

A must try!

1 pound hamburger
1 clove garlic, minced
2 teaspoons sugar
1 teaspoon salt
¼ teaspoon black pepper
2 8-ounce cans tomato sauce **OR**
1 8-ounce can whole tomatoes and
1 8-ounce can tomato sauce
1 8-ounce package cream cheese
1 cup sour cream
6 green onions (including the green part), chopped
1 8-ounce package lasagna noodles
1 cup grated Cheddar cheese

Preheat oven to 350 degrees. Lightly grease a 9-inch by 13-inch baking dish.

In a large skillet, brown hamburger over medium heat. Drain off any fat. Add garlic, sugar, salt, pepper and tomato sauce; reduce heat to medium-low and simmer 20 minutes.

In a large bowl, combine cream cheese, sour cream and chopped green onions and mix until smooth. Cook lasagna noodles according to directions and drain.

Place a layer of cooked lasagna noodles in the bottom of prepared baking dish; then a layer of cream cheese mixture; then a layer of meat sauce. Repeat layers, ending with lasagna noodles. Sprinkle Cheddar cheese on top. Bake for about 20 minutes or until heated through and bubbly.

Dotti Wilson

▪ PEROGI ▪

Dough:

3 cups flour
½ teaspoon salt
1 cup milk
1 egg, beaten

Filling:

3 cups hot mashed potatoes
1 cup drained cottage cheese
Salt and pepper to taste

Sauce:

5 slices bacon; cooked until crisp and crumbled
1 medium onion, finely chopped
1 cup sliced mushrooms
½ cup butter

For the Dough:

In a large bowl, stir together the flour and salt. Combine milk and beaten egg and stir into flour. Stir vigorously until smooth. Turn out dough onto a lightly floured surface and knead until smooth and elastic, about 3 minutes. Divide dough in half. Dust with flour, cover with plastic wrap and allow to rest for 30 minutes before rolling.

For the Filling:

The night before preparing Perogi, drain cottage cheese by placing cottage cheese in a colander lined with cheesecloth. Cover with plastic wrap. Place colander in a bowl to catch whey and refrigerate overnight. The following day discard whey.

Place hot mashed potatoes in a large bowl and stir in drained cottage cheese. Season well with salt and pepper. Allow to cool completely.

For the Sauce:

Dice bacon and fry in a large skillet over medium heat until crisp. Remove bacon with a slotted spoon and set aside. Discard all but 1 tablespoon bacon drippings. Add onions to skillet and sauté until translucent. Add mushrooms and sauté until tender. Return bacon to pan and add butter. As soon as butter is melted, remove from heat. Pour Sauce into a large serving bowl, set aside and keep warm.

To assemble and cook Perogi:

On a lightly floured surface, roll out dough until ¼-inch thick. Cut into circles using a 2½-inch diameter cookie cutter or glass. Place 2 teaspoons filling in the center and fold dough in half to enclose filling completely. Press edges together to seal well. Place Perogi, in one layer, on a lightly floured surface. Make sure that they don't touch each other or they will stick. Repeat until all dough and filling are used.

Bring a large pot of salted water to a boil. Add 1 tablespoon of oil to water to prevent Perogi from sticking together. Add Perogi to pot, a few at a time, stirring gently to prevent sticking. Perogi will sink, then float. Cook for about 3 to 5 minutes. When they float remove them with a slotted spoon and drain. Place the cooked Perogi in the warm sauce. Repeat until all Perogi are cooked and coated in the sauce. Serve with a dollop of sour cream if desired.

Helen McChrystal

> "And as surely as gravity will compress a dying star until it is crushed to oblivion, it's unstoppable force will compress the Universe, shrink it until all matter—*everything*—falls together into one, single, infinitely small point. And *then*—"
>
> *—Oregon Symphony Director James DePriest, from the Kendall Planetarium show Cosmic Fury*
>
> *Mark Bourne*

▪ BUTTERNUT SQUASH RAVIOLI WITH HAZELNUT AND SAGE BUTTER SAUCE ▪

Butternut Squash Ravioli:

1 butternut squash
1 tablespoon olive oil
1 small onion, finely chopped
8 ounces ricotta cheese
1 egg
⅛ teaspoon nutmeg
Salt and pepper to taste
1½ pounds fresh pasta sheets

Hazelnut and Sage Butter Sauce:

1 tablespoon olive oil
½ cup toasted hazelnuts, chopped
1 tablespoon shallot, minced
¼ cup Marsala wine
½ cup unsalted butter
1 tablespoon fresh sage, minced
Salt and pepper to taste
Freshly grated Parmesan cheese

Preheat oven to 400 degrees.

For the Butternut Squash Ravioli:

Place squash in a baking pan and bake for 40 minutes, or until very tender. Cool and discard seeds and skin. Heat 1 tablespoon olive oil in a sauté pan, over medium heat, and sauté onion for about 10 minutes, or until very tender. When completely cool combine with squash, ricotta, egg, nutmeg, salt and pepper in the bowl of a food processor and process for 1 minute.

Place a fresh pasta sheet on a lightly floured surface. Place 1 tablespoon of butternut squash filling at regular intervals, with 1-inch spaces apart on all sides. With a small brush dipped in water, moisten pasta around the fillings. Place a slightly larger sheet of pasta over the first, and press down gently around the fillings. Using a ravioli cutter, pastry wheel or sharp knife, separate the ravioli. Place in one layer on well-floured baking sheets, taking care that they don't touch.

For the Hazelnut and Sage Butter Sauce:

Heat 1 tablespoon olive oil in a sauté pan over medium-low heat. Sauté the hazelnuts and shallots for 2 minutes. Add the Marsala and reduce by half. Add sage, salt and pepper. Reduce heat to low and whisk in cold butter, 1 tablespoon at a time, whisking constantly until smooth.

Bring a large pot of salted water to a boil. Add ravioli, a few at a time to boiling water, do not crowd. Cook for about 2 minutes or until al dente. Drain and serve tossed with Hazelnut and Sage Butter Sauce and sprinkle with Parmesan.

David Machado
Pazzo Ristorante
Portland, Oregon

> ***Why does soda pop "feel" so good?***
>
> Well, it's because of the type of sugar used to sweeten it. Rather than use a complex sugar like sucrose (table sugar), the soft drink manufacturer uses a simple sugar called fructose. This fruit sugar is so easily digested and taken-up by the blood stream that we literally "feel" the rush of sweetener moving through our body before finishing the drink. It's no wonder we become loyal to our favorite brand!
>
> *David Heil*
> *Newton's Apple*
> *Associate Director, OMSI*

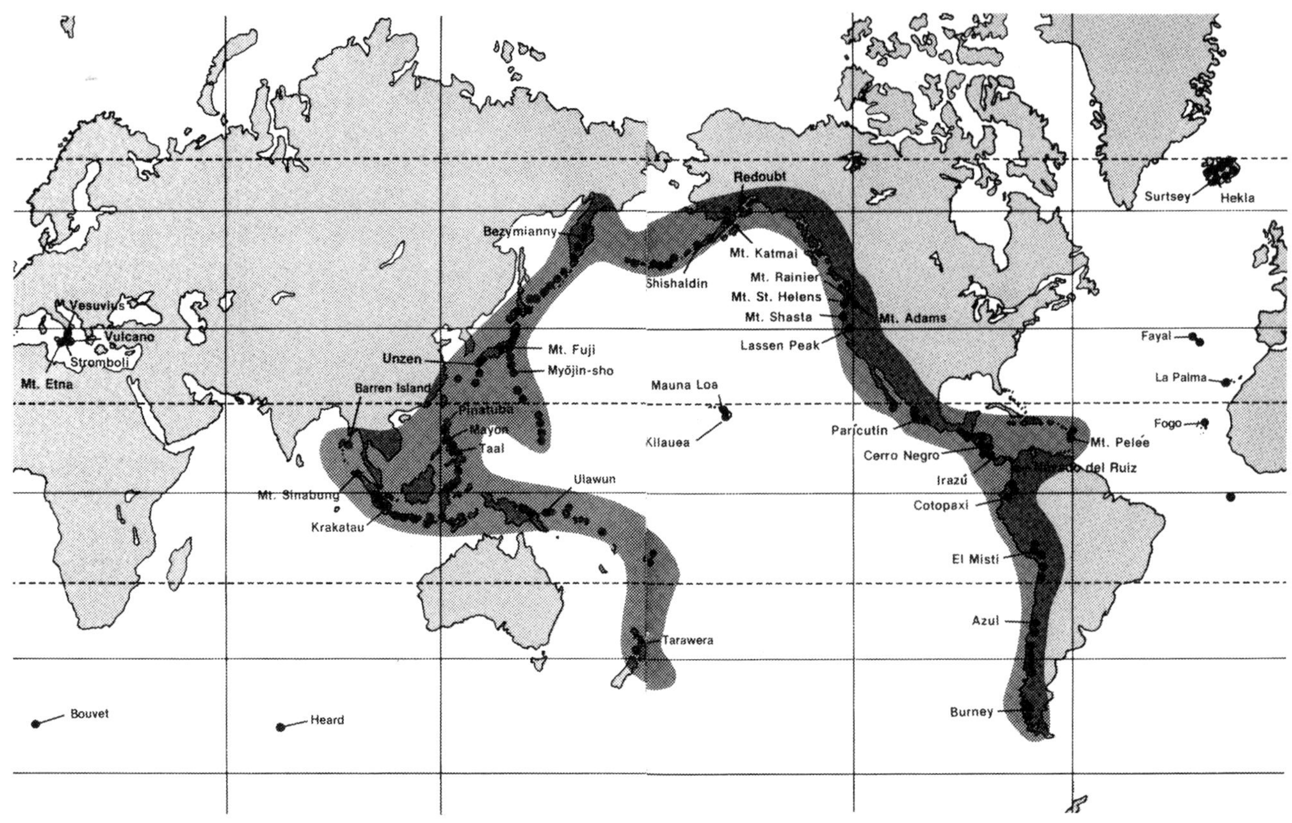

The Ring of Fire

There are more than 500 active volcanoes (those that have erupted at least once within recorded history) in the world—50 of which are in the United States (Hawaii, Alaska, Washington, Oregon and California)—although many more are hidden under the seas. Most are strung like beads along, or near, the margins of the continents, and more than half encircle the Pacific Ocean as a "Ring of Fire."

▪ SPAGHETTI WITH EGGPLANT SAUCE ▪

2 tablespoons olive oil
3 large cloves garlic, minced
2 pounds ripe Roma tomatoes, seeded and quartered
¾ cup water
¼ cup fresh basil, finely chopped
¼ cup fresh parsley, finely chopped
Salt and pepper to taste
4 tablespoons olive oil
2 pounds eggplant, peeled and diced into ½-inch cubes
12 ounces spaghetti
1 cup fresh Parmesan, grated

In a large pot, heat 2 tablespoons olive oil over medium heat. Add garlic and sauté until fragrant. Add tomatoes, water, basil, parsley, salt and pepper. Reduce heat to low and simmer, stirring occasionally, for 30 minutes.

In a large non-stick skillet, heat remaining 4 tablespoons olive oil over medium heat. Add eggplant and brown evenly on all sides. Add eggplant to sauce, cover and simmer an additional 30 minutes, stirring often so sauce doesn't scorch.

Cook and drain spaghetti and toss with Eggplant Sauce. Sprinkle with Parmesan cheese and serve immediately. Serves 4.

Jim and Karen Bosley

▪ GRANCHIO ALLA PANNA ▪

- 2 tablespoons unsalted butter
- 1½ to 2 cups heavy cream
- Juice of ½ lemon
- 1 tablespoon dry dill
- 10 ounces fresh Dungeness crab meat
- ½ bunch fresh spinach, washed and dried
- Salt and pepper to taste
- ½ pound fresh linguine, cooked al dente

In a heavy, non-reactive (stainless steel or enamel) skillet, melt butter over medium heat. Add cream, lemon juice and dill and increase heat to medium-high. Reduce by half, whisking often. Stir in the crab and spinach and simmer until crab is heated through and spinach is wilted. Season to taste with salt and pepper.

Toss sauce with the cooked linguine. Garnish with fresh dill or parsley and lemon wedges, if desired. Serves 2.

Joy Graham
Delfinia's Pasta
and Pizza
Portland, Oregon

▪ SPAGHETTI CASSEROLE ▪

My Mother taught me to make this many years ago and it has been a family favorite since then. This can be used as a side dish, or if made in larger quantities, it makes a fantastic entree. I have one friend who will even eat it for breakfast, if there is any left over. I hope you like it as much as we do!

- ½ to ¾ pound spaghetti, cooked in salted water until tender then drained
- 4 tablespoons margarine **OR** butter
- 1 large onion, chopped
- 1 1-pound 13-ounce can whole tomatoes

Preheat oven to 300 degrees. Lightly grease a 3-quart casserole dish.

Melt 2 tablespoons of the margarine in a skillet over medium heat. Add onions and sauté until translucent. Put onions in prepared casserole dish. Lightly break up the tomatoes and stir into the onions. Stir in the cooked and drained spaghetti. Dot with remaining margarine. Bake for about 1 hour.

Lois Hall

SEAFOOD

▪ Science Camps ▪

Another arm of OMSI considers time on a slower scale than the sometimes frenetic pace of technology. Researchers and students in these programs investigate how long a fossil takes to form, the rate of moving water in a river, or how fast a kangaroo rat can hop. Youngsters find out why whales are warm blooded and fish aren't, why fossils of palm trees and ferns are found in the Central Oregon desert, and why less rain falls in Eastern rather than Western Oregon. These questions are asked and answered daily at OMSI's natural science camps at the coast and in Central Oregon.

As in all of it's activities, OMSI camps are structured to totally engage the participant in natural science intellectually, physically, and emotionally. Animals are touched, fossils are dug, geological processes are viewed and sometimes recreated in miniature. The whole outdoors is the classroom. Although recreation and arts and crafts are a part of camp life, at OMSI camps, the fun is found in science also.

OMSI programs take place at several camps around the state: Camp Kiwanilong near Warrenton, Oregon, on the northern coast; Hancock Field Station near Fossil, Oregon, in Central Oregon; and Cascade Science School near Bend, Oregon, in the Cascade Mountains. But the learning of science is not limited to these areas; Campers kayak in the San Juan Islands, backpack through Yellowstone National Park and the Grand Canyon; investigate the South Slough Estuary near Coos Bay, Oregon; and climb to the rim of Mount St. Helens to look down into the awe-inspiring crater formed in 1980. These trips give the campers a broader look at their world, a way to explore career opportunities, and an opportunity to expand their thinking.

During the summer these camp programs run from one to two weeks for children ages 7 to 18. The campers come from throughout the country, with the majority from the Willamette Valley. Buses pick them up and return them to OMSI's Education Resource Center.

During the spring and fall students from first grade through college graduates come to these sites with their teachers for several days to a week of intensive science instruction provided by OMSI's professional teaching staff. All the instructors have graduate or undergraduate degrees in one of the natural sciences.

Several weekends a year families are invited to OMSI's residential camps to participate in a variety of natural history programs from paleontology, to marine ecology and astronomy. These two to three day programs draw all ages from toddlers to grandparents with activities planned to accommodate the energy levels and interests of each age.

Connie Hofferber Jones

▪ OYSTERS FLORENTINE ▪

1 10-ounce package frozen spinach
2 6-ounce jars of oysters
1 tablespoon butter
1 clove garlic
¼ cup cream cheese
¼ cup sour cream
Dash of Worcestershire sauce
Salt and pepper to taste
⅛ cup Parmesan cheese, grated
½ cup Cheddar cheese, grated
Sprinkle of paprika

Cook spinach according to the directions, drain, and set aside. Sauté drained oysters in hot butter and garlic for about 2 minutes. Add cream cheese and melt over medium heat. Add sour cream, Worcestershire sauce, salt, pepper, and Parmesan cheese. Place cooked spinach in a small casserole dish or individual soufflé dishes. Spoon the oysters and sauce over the spinach. Sprinkle Cheddar cheese over mixture. Sprinkle with paprika. Bake about 5 to 7 minutes at 325 degrees, or until cheese has melted and the dish is heated thoroughly. Serve with hot buttered French bread and your favorite white wine. Serves two.

Eadi Popick
Bruce Spainhower

Lon Hancock, founder of Camp Hancock, with the skull of the extinct rhinoceros Amynodon.

▪ PRAWNS FOSSI ▪

"Fossi" means awesome, intergalactically incredible, excellent. I'm sure you will find this prawn recipe simply fossinating with flavor guaranteed to send your taste buds into outer space!

2 dozen large prawns
4 tablespoons butter
1 tablespoon olive oil
Juice of 2 lemons
1 tablespoon dry white wine
1 teaspoon Greek oregano
Salt and pepper to taste

Shell and devein prawns. Heat butter and olive oil in a large sauté pan or skillet over medium heat. Add prawns and sauté just until they start to turn pink. Add lemon juice, wine, oregano, salt and pepper and continue to sauté until prawns are cooked.

Dwon Paul O'Dell
(The Original Fossinator)

What Ever Happened to the Two-Headed Lamb?

A mounted lamb with two faces, two tails, and an extra leg or two, this popular exhibit provided a real-life illustration of a genetic anomaly. The lamb is now back at the new museum with the return of the Designer Genes exhibit.

▪ BRUNCH SOUFFLÉ ▪

This is a perfect dish to make ahead.

- 8 ounces French bread, torn into bite-sized pieces
- 3 tablespoons melted butter
- ¾ pound Swiss cheese, shredded
- ½ pound Monterey Jack cheese, shredded
- 1 cup cooked crab meat **OR** cooked shrimp **OR** cooked and crumbled bacon
- 12 eggs, lightly beaten
- ¾ cup milk
- ⅓ cup dry white wine
- 2 green onions including the green tops, chopped
- ¾ teaspoon Dijon mustard
- ¼ teaspoon white pepper
- ¾ cup sour cream
- ½ cup Parmesan cheese, grated
- Paprika

Lightly butter a 9-inch by 13-inch baking dish.

Place bread pieces in prepared baking dish. Drizzle over melted butter. Layer on Swiss cheese, Monterey Jack and meat of your choice. In a medium bowl, combine eggs, milk, white wine, green onions, Dijon and white pepper and mix well. Pour egg mixture over bread. Cover tightly with aluminum foil and refrigerate overnight.

The following day, remove from refrigerator and allow to sit at room temperature for 30 minutes before baking. Preheat oven to 325 degrees.

Bake covered casserole for 1 hour. Remove from oven, uncover and allow to cool for 5 minutes.

Stir together sour cream and Parmesan and spread mixture on top of casserole. Sprinkle with paprika for color. Return to oven, uncovered, and bake and additional 10 minutes, or until golden brown. Serves 8.

Corky Poppert

▪ LUTEFISK ▪

(THE POOR MANS' LOBSTER)

- Lutefisk
- Melted butter

Boiled Lutefisk:

Take one frozen lutefisk and thaw to room temperature. Place in rapidly boiling water. Reduce heat to medium and simmer until fish flakes easily. Drain and serve with melted butter.

Baked Lutefisk:

Preheat oven to 350 degrees.

Take one frozen lutefisk and thaw to room temperature. Place in baking dish. Bake for about 20 to 30 minutes, or until fish flakes easily. Serve with melted butter.

Francis C. Berg

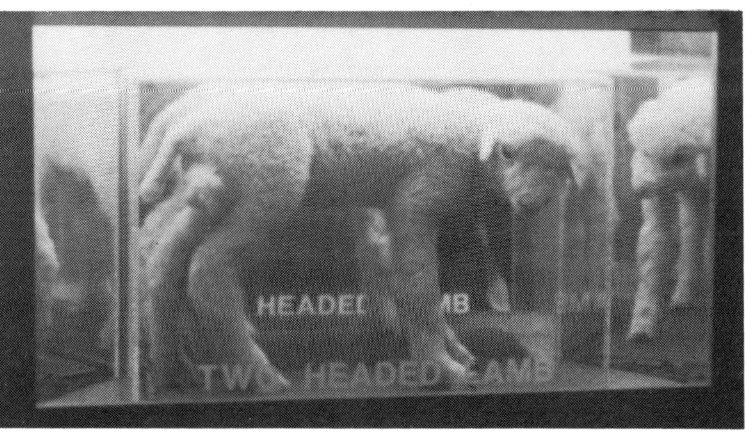

▪ SHOALWATER SALMON ▪

I devised this recipe one September evening on the Long Beach Peninsula when the salmon was good and inexpensive and it was my turn to cook.

2 salmon filets
4 whole peppercorns
2 teaspoons fresh dill
4 lemon slices
Water
2 tablespoon butter
⅓ to ½ cup red bell pepper, thinly sliced lengthwise
½ cup dry white wine
⅓ cup cream
1 teaspoon fresh dill **OR** ¼ teaspoon dry dill
Salt and pepper to taste

Place peppercorns, 2 teaspoons dill and lemon slices in a large skillet. Add enough water to come up halfway. Bring water to a simmer over medium-low heat. Add salmon filets and poach until fish flakes easily. Remove salmon and keep warm.

In a large skillet, heat butter over medium heat. Add bell peppers and sauté until tender. Add wine and reduce by half. Whisk in cream and simmer until sauce coats the back of a spoon. Whisk in 1 teaspoon dill, salt and pepper. Spoon sauce over salmon filets. Serves 2.

Leo MacLeod

Why is the Ocean Salty?

Sea water has been defined as a weak solution of almost everything. Ocean water is indeed a complex solution of mineral salts and of decayed biologic matter that results from the sea teeming with life. Most of the ocean's salts were derived from gradual processes such as the breaking up of the cooled igneous rocks of the Earth's crust by weathering and erosion, the wearing down of mountains, and the dissolving action of rains and streams which transported their mineral washings to the sea. Some of the ocean's salts have been dissolved from rocks and sediments below its floor. Other sources of salts include the solid and gaseous materials that escaped from the Earth's crust through volcanic vents or that originated in the atmosphere. The average salinity of sea water is 35 0/00 or 35 pounds of salt per 1,000 pounds of water. Sodium and chloride constitute 85 percent of the dissolved solids in sea water and account for the characteristic salty taste.

If the salt in the sea could be removed and spread evenly over the Earth's land surface it would form a layer more than 500 feet thick.

▪ SMOKED SALMON ▪

Eddie Wied is one of the greatest Jazz Pianists around. He can also master the "smoker" like the piano keys he is so respectfully known for. This is his recipe and it always gets rave reviews.

3 salmon fillets
2 quarts water
1 cup brown sugar
¾ cup kosher salt
2 to 3 bay leaves
Pure maple syrup
Apple and cherry wood chips

In a large stainless steel, or other non-reactive bowl, whisk together water, brown sugar, salt and bay leaves. Remove all bones from fish and rinse. Place salmon in brine and weight down with a plate. Cover with plastic wrap and refrigerate overnight.

The next day remove salmon from brine and rinse well. Pat dry. Allow salmon to air-dry for about 1 hour. Preheat smoker according to manufacturer's directions. Oil racks. Place salmon on racks and brush with maple syrup. Cover smoker and smoke for about 10 to 12 hours. Restock wood chips when needed. I use 3 pans of wood chips for this amount of salmon.

Patricia Wied

Solar System

To get a sense of the relative sizes of certain features of the solar system, imagine the Sun as a sphere as tall as you are. Then the largest planet, Jupiter, would be smaller than your head, the Earth would be the size of the iris of your eye, and Mercury the size of your pupil.

We use the human body again to get a sense of planetary orbits. If you stand with your arms outstretched and imagine the tip of your right hand touching Pluto and the tip of your left hand touching the Sun, then the orbits of the inner planets are all in your finger: Mercury between the tip and first knuckle, the orbit of Venus lies in the middle of your finger, the orbit of Earth passes through the middle knuckle, and the orbit of Mars lies at the base of your finger. Jupiter is at your wrist, the orbit of Saturn passes through your elbow, while that of Uranus is in the vicinity of your neck, the orbit of Neptune at your right elbow and, of course, the tip of your finger touches Pluto. On this scale the Sun, at the tip of your left hand, is a small grain of sand.

Scott MacGregor

▪ CRAWFISH BOIL ▪

20 pounds live crawfish
Water to cover
1 pound salt, to purge
Water to cover
1 pound salt, to cook
6 to 8 onions, quartered
6 to 8 lemons, sliced
3 bags crab boil (I use Zatarain's)
1 bottle crab boil (I use Zatarain's)
3 ounces cayenne
4 cloves garlic, minced

Place crawfish in a very large pot. Cover crawfish with water and stir in 1 pound of salt. Soak for 30 minutes to purge crawfish. Drain. Cover again with fresh water and stir in 1 pound salt. Add remaining ingredients. Bring to a boil and boil for 15 minutes. Remove from heat and let stand for 30 minutes to 1 hour, depending how spicy you want them. Peel and enjoy!

Leo and Susan Provencher

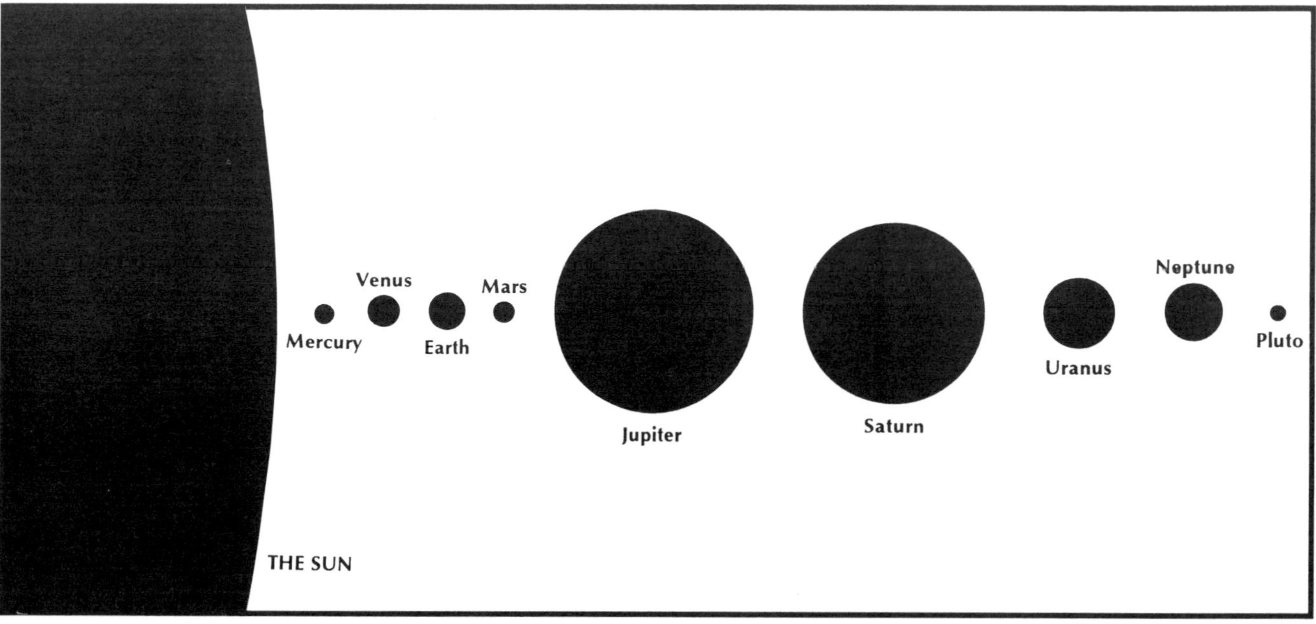

▪ STUFFED CRAB ▪

3 tablespoons butter
1 large onion, finely chopped
2 ribs celery, finely chopped
4 green onions, finely chopped
½ green bell pepper, finely chopped
1 teaspoon garlic, minced
1 teaspoon Creole seasoning
½ teaspoon thyme
½ teaspoon Worcestershire sauce
1 bay leaf, crumbled
⅛ teaspoon cayenne
Salt and pepper to taste
1 pound crab meat
½ loaf stale bread crumbs, slightly dampened with water
2 eggs, beaten
1 tablespoon fresh parsley, minced
Additional bread crumbs
Butter
Crab shells

Preheat oven to 350 degrees.

Heat 3 tablespoons butter in a large skillet over medium heat. Add onion, celery, green onions, green pepper and garlic and sauté until tender. Reduce heat to low and add Creole seasoning, thyme, Worcestershire sauce, bay leaf, salt and pepper to taste and simmer for 15 minutes. Remove from heat and stir in crab meat, eggs and parsley. Place about ⅓ cup stuffing into crab shells, sprinkle with bread crumbs and dot with butter. Place stuffed crab shells on a baking sheet and bake for about 30 minutes, or until golden brown.

Pat Shumard

▪ SHRIMP AND OYSTER JAMBALAYA ▪

4 tablespoons butter
1 cup ham, diced
1 cup onion, diced
¾ cup green bell pepper, diced
1 clove garlic, minced
1½ cups boiling water
2 chicken bouillon cubes
1½ teaspoons salt
½ teaspoon thyme
¼ teaspoon cayenne pepper
⅛ teaspoon cloves
⅛ teaspoon nutmeg
¼ cup fresh parsley, minced
3½ cups tomatoes; peeled, seeded and chopped
1½ pounds shrimp, peeled and deveined
1 pint oysters, with their liquid
6 cups cooked white rice

In a large skillet, melt butter over medium heat. Add ham, onion, bell pepper and garlic and sauté until vegetables are tender. Set aside.

In a large pot combine boiling water and chicken bouillon cubes. Add salt, thyme, cayenne, cloves, nutmeg, parsley and tomatoes and bring to a boil. Reduce heat to medium-low and simmer for 10 minutes. Add shrimp and oysters and simmer an additional 3 minutes. Stir in cooked rice and reserved vegetable mixture. Bring to a boil then remove from heat, cover and let stand for 5 minutes before serving.

Jim, Mary and Chelsea Fredrick

"Here, imbedded deep within the universe, we can look out into our galaxy and beyond, into a cosmos filled with amazing places and breathtaking scenery. Just think of the night sky as a map, a map where uncountable worlds lead to vistas of unearthly beauty and wonder. All you have to do is look up, and hitch a ride on your imagination. We guarantee you'll have a good trip."

—the Cruise Guide
played by Kim Sherwood,
from the Murdock Sky Theater
show Dream Worlds, Inc.

Mark Bourne

▪ TUNA WITH MADEIRA, ORANGE AND SOY ▪

This unusual combination of ingredients makes for a surprising and delicious sauce that suits fresh tuna. Madeira is a fortified wine similar to sherry, which can be used as a substitute although it is not as full flavored.

4 medallions of yellowfin tuna,
  3 to 4 ounces each
½ cup flour
2 tablespoons salad oil
1 tablespoon soy sauce
¼ cup Madeira
¼ cup orange juice
¼ cup cream
2 tablespoons butter

Preheat oven to 200 degrees.

Dust tuna medallions with flour and shake off excess. Heat oil over medium heat in a sauté pan large enough to hold medallions. Sauté for 2 minutes on each side, until browned. Remove to ovenproof dish and keep warm in the oven.

Pour off and wipe out any excess oil from the pan and return to the heat. Combine remaining ingredients, except the butter, and boil to reduce by half. Remove sauce from heat and swirl in the butter until just melted and blended in the sauce.

Place tuna medallions on dinner plates and pour sauce over them. Serves 2. Approximate preparation time: 15 minutes.

Jake's Seafood Cookbook

Which came first, the chicken or the egg?

Eggs came first. The first eggs laid on land were produced by reptiles 250 million years ago. Domesticated chickens have only been around for 5 thousand years.

David Heil
Newton's Apple
Associate Director, OMSI

▪ SWORDFISH TERIYAKI ▪

This Teriyaki Sauce is also excellent on chicken.

1 15-ounce can crushed pineapple
1½ cups soy sauce
¾ cup brown sugar
1 tablespoon garlic, minced
1 tablespoon fresh ginger, grated
½ teaspoon curry powder
1 pound swordfish, cut into bite-sized
  pieces

Drain pineapple and reserve the juice and 2 tablespoons of the pineapple. Save the remaining pineapple for another use.

Place pineapple juice, 2 tablespoons crushed pineapple, soy sauce, brown sugar, garlic, ginger and curry powder in a sauce pan. Bring to a boil, stirring constantly. Reduce heat to medium and cook until sugar is dissolved and mixture has thickened slightly, about 10 minutes. Pour sauce into a skillet and bring to a simmer over medium heat. Add swordfish and simmer, stirring constantly, until fish is cooked through. Serve with plain white rice and pass remaining sauce.

Anthony Edward Burger

▪ SWORDFISH CASINO ▪

Swordfish has become a luxury these days as the price moves out of sight. When you add crab meat, you're likely to break the bank. But if you've got someone you really want to impress, and money's no object, here's a classy recipe from Chef Whitney Peterson at McCormick's Fish House in Beaverton, Oregon, for a very special dinner party.

¼ cup Beurre Blanc Sauce (See recipe, page 61)
2 swordfish steaks, 1-inch thick, 5 to 6 ounces each
3 ounces dungeness crab meat
2 tablespoons roasted red peppers, julienne cut, (See **NOTE**)
1 teaspoon lemon juice
2 tablespoons fresh basil leaves, finely shredded
Pinch salt
Pinch pepper

Preheat oven to 400 degrees.

Prepare the Beurre Blanc Sauce and set aside.

Cut a slit in the swordfish steaks to form a pocket, as you might for stuffed pork chops.

Combine crab, roasted red peppers, lemon juice, basil, salt and pepper to make the stuffing. Divide between the pockets of the 2 steaks.

If you have a range-top system like a Jenn-Air, you can "mark" the swordfish with the grill's crosshatching. Marked or not, bake in the oven for 10 minutes.

Remove to dinner plates and coat each steak with 2 tablespoons Beurre Blanc Sauce. Serves 2. Approximate preparation time: 20 minutes.

NOTE: Roasted red peppers are readily available in supermarkets.

Jake's Seafood Cookbook

▪ PECAN CATFISH WITH HONEY LEMON CHILI BUTTER ▪

Using chopped nuts to coat fish before cooking is a great way to add flavor and texture to your meal. When pan-frying a nut-coated fish, you must take care to keep the heat moderate so you don't burn it. Chef Whitney Peterson of McCormick's Fish House in Beaverton, Oregon, finishes this fish with a trio of sweet, tart and spicy flavors.

2 catfish filets, 6 to 8 ounces each
1 cup pecans
1 cup flour
1 egg beaten with 1 tablespoon milk
3 tablespoons oil for frying
4 tablespoons chicken stock
1 tablespoon honey
1 tablespoon lemon juice
¼ teaspoon crushed red chili pepper flakes
1 tablespoon melted butter
1 teaspoon fresh parsley, minced

Trim any loose pieces from the catfish filets.

Chop the pecans very fine.

Set up 3 baking dishes or pie pans on your counter and put flour in the first pan, beaten egg mixture in the second and chopped pecans in the third. Bread the filets by coating lightly in flour, shaking off the excess. Dip in the egg mixture and finally coat them in the nuts, pressing the pecans into the filets on both sides.

Heat oil in a large pan. Pan-fry the catfish over medium-high heat, for 3 to 4 minutes per side. If the coating gets too brown too quickly, remove filets to a pie pan and finish them in a 400 degree oven for 3 to 4 minutes. Combine the remaining ingredients for the sauce and set aside.

Place the cooked catfish on dinner plates and pour the sauce over them. Serves 2. Approximate preparation time: 20 minutes.

Jake's Seafood Cookbook

▪ SEAFOOD CHILI ▪

At first you might be somewhat skeptical about the wisdom of serving chili made with seafood, but don't knock it until you've tried it. This chili from Chef Rene VanBroekhuizen is great! The flavors blend nicely and it doesn't overpower the fish. Most shellfish and fish work in this recipe, which is great for lunch, dinner or reheated as leftovers.

1 cup dry black beans
3 tablespoons olive oil
1 cup onion, diced
1 cup red and/or green pepper, diced
1 small jalapeno, minced
2 teaspoons chipotle pepper puree (See **NOTE**.)
1 teaspoon cumin
1 teaspoon chili powder
1 teaspoon onion powder
½ teaspoon oregano
½ teaspoon salt
1 teaspoon black pepper
1 cup chicken stock, commercial or homemade
1 28-ounce can diced tomato
1 pound bay shrimp
1½ pounds fish filet (cod, sea bass, rockfish, etc.), diced
8-ounces cheddar or jack cheese, shredded
1 bunch cilantro, chopped or sprigs
Assorted hot or mild peppers, for garnish
1 cup fresh Tomato **OR** Papaya **OR** Avocado salsa (See recipes, pages 6-7)
6 large flour tortillas, rolled and halved for garnish

Soak the black beans overnight. Drain. Cook the beans in fresh water until very tender. Drain and reserve.

In a large saucepan, heat 1 tablespoon of the oil over medium heat. Add the next ten ingredients and cook for 4 or 5 minutes. Add the chicken stock and tomatoes, reduce the heat to low and simmer 20 minutes.

Heat the remaining oil in another saucepan and sauté the seafood for 2 to 3 minutes.

Add the chili sauce and black beans to the seafood and cook an additional 1 to 2 minutes.

Spoon the chili into bowls and top with the cheese. Garnish with the cilantro, peppers, salsa and flour tortillas. Serves 4 to 6.

Approximate preparation time: Soak beans overnight; 1 hour preparation time.

NOTE: Canned chipotle peppers are available in specialty and Mexican groceries. Oriental hot chili paste also works.

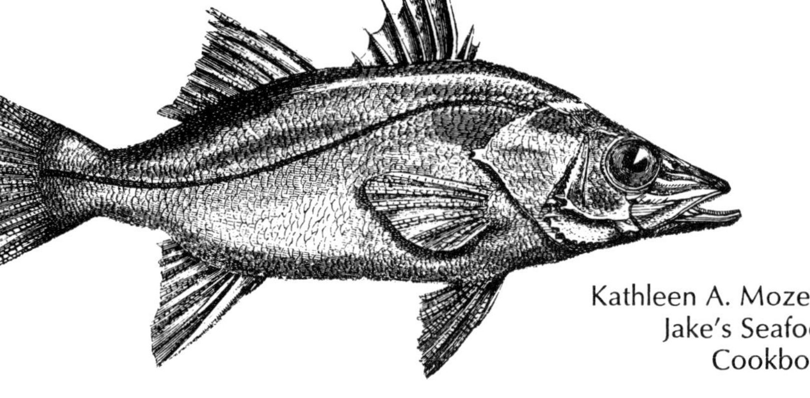

Kathleen A. Mozena
Jake's Seafood Cookbook

▪ LEMON AND THYME MARINADE ▪

This is great for scallops, shrimp, fish, chicken or lamb.

½ cup fresh lemon juice
¼ cup minced shallots
¼ cup fresh thyme leaves, minced
4½ teaspoons lemon zest, minced
2 teaspoons salt
1 teaspoon black pepper
½ cup vegetable oil

In a large bowl, combine together lemon juice, shallots, thyme, lemon zest, salt and pepper. Stir until the salt is dissolved. Whisk in the oil in a thin stream. Makes 1⅓ cups.

Toni J. Ives

▪ BEURRE BLANC SAUCE ▪

6 ounces white wine
3 ounces white wine vinegar
3 whole peppercorns
1 shallot, cut into quarters
1 cup heavy cream
6 ounces cold, unsalted butter, cut into pieces
3 ounces cold butter, cut into pieces

Combine wine, vinegar, peppercorns and shallot in a noncorrosive saucepan (stainless steel, teflon, calphalon).

Reduce until the mixture is just 1 to 2 tablespoons and has the consistency of syrup.

Add cream and reduce again until mixture is 3 to 4 tablespoons and very syrupy. Remove from heat.

Add butters, about 2 ounces at a time, stirring constantly and allowing each addition to melt in before adding more. (If mixture cools too much, butter will not melt completely and you will have to reheat slightly.)

Strain and hold warm on a stove-top trivet or in a double-boiler over very low heat until you are ready to use it.

NOTE: This sauce may be flavored with orange, lemon, spices, herbs, berry or fruit concentrates. These may be added at the end or during the reduction of the cream.

Makes about 1 cup.

Whitney Petersen
Jake's Famous Crayfish
Portland, Oregon

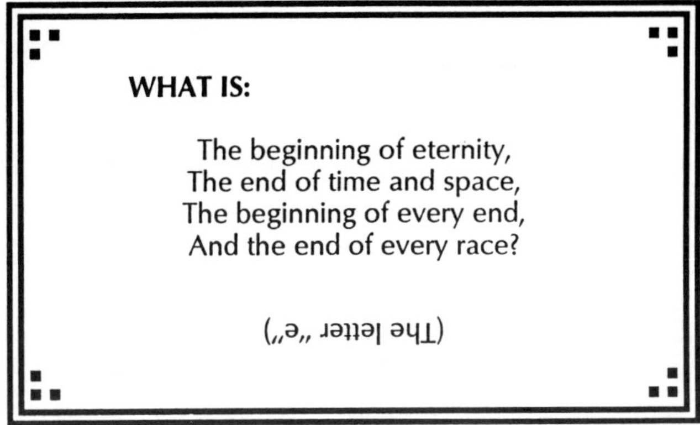

WHAT IS:

The beginning of eternity,
The end of time and space,
The beginning of every end,
And the end of every race?

(The letter "e")

POULTRY

▪ Cascade Science School ▪

OMSI's newest program is located in the Cascade Mountains with headquarters at the historic Skyliner Lodge, 10 miles west of Bend, Oregon on Tumalo Creek. Located in the Deschutes National Forest, the former ski area and lodge offer an excellent location for studying forest and stream ecology, cultural history, astronomy, and Cascades geology. The facility is rustic with screened, open air cabins, outhouses, and an impressive stone and timber lodge with a massive stone fireplace. Dining facilities and meeting rooms are located in the lodge.

Cascade Science School is a continuation of OMSI programs in the Bend area that began 25 years ago with backpacking programs into the high Cascades. With the lease of Skyliner Lodge in 1993, these Cascade programs have a local base of operation. In addition to the residential spring, fall and summer programs, Cascade Science School provides summer day camp for La Pine, Bend and Redmond area youngsters at local parks and recreation areas in geology, forest and stream ecology and wilderness skills.

OMSI camps immerse people in a positive and wholesome learning environment. Self-esteem, confidence, and friendships develop naturally where adventure and activity are balanced with quiet and reflective moments.

Connie Hofferber Jones

▪ CHICKEN PICCATA ▪

2 whole chicken breasts; halved, skinned and boned
Flour
1 tablespoon olive oil
1 tablespoon butter
1 clove garlic, minced
1 cup dry white wine **OR** dry vermouth
2 to 3 tablespoons lemon juice
1 tablespoon capers
2 tablespoons fresh parsley, minced

Pound chicken breasts to ¼-inch thick. Dredge in flour and shake off excess. Heat olive oil and butter together in a large skillet over medium heat. Add garlic and sauté until fragrant. Add chicken and brown on both sides. Remove and keep warm. Add wine, lemon juice, capers and parsley and simmer until reduced by half. Return chicken to pan and heat through. Serves 2.

Leo MacLeod

▪ STIR-FRIED CHICKEN ▪

¼ cup honey
¼ cup water
2 tablespoons dry sherry
2 tablespoons soy sauce
1 tablespoon cornstarch
1 clove garlic, minced
¼ teaspoon ground ginger
2 tablespoons corn oil
2 whole boneless, skinless chicken breasts, cut into ½-inch pieces
2 small tomatoes, cut into wedges
1 small green bell pepper, seeded and cut into ½-inch pieces

In a small bowl, stir together honey, water, sherry, soy sauce, cornstarch, garlic and ginger and set aside. In a large wok or skillet, heat oil over medium-high heat. Add chicken and stir-fry for about 3 minutes or until chicken is cooked. Add tomato and green pepper. Add honey mixture and bring to a boil, stirring constantly, and cook until sauce has thickened, about 1 minute. Serve over rice.

Dotti Wilson

▪ EINSTEIN'S CHICKEN AND DUMPLINGS ▪

Albert Einstein's birthday is March 14, or 3.14. . . pi, more or less. His favorite meal was Chicken and Dumplings and Cherry Pie (try Einstein pi on page 119). Serve this to celebrate his birthday.

1 cup flour
2 teaspoons paprika
2 teaspoons salt
¼ teaspoon pepper
2 tablespoons vegetable oil
1 4-pound chicken, cut into serving pieces
1 small onion, chopped
1 carrot, chopped
1 stalk celery, chopped
1 cup water
3 tablespoons butter, softened
2½ cups milk

Dumplings:

1½ cups flour
2 teaspoons baking powder
½ teaspoon salt
3 tablespoons shortening
¾ cup milk

In a shallow dish mix flour, paprika, salt and pepper with a fork. Reserve 3 tablespoons of this mixture. Dredge chicken pieces in flour mixture. Heat oil in a Dutch oven or large pot over medium heat. Brown chicken on all sides. Add onion, carrot and celery and sauté until tender. Add water, cover tightly and reduce heat to low. Cook for about 2 hours or until chicken is very tender. Add water if necessary.

When chicken is done, remove from pot and keep warm. Skim off fat from liquid in pot. Mix reserved 3 tablespoons flour mixture with the softened butter until a smooth paste is formed. Whisk mixture into the liquid in the pot until well blended. Increase heat to medium-high and whisk in milk in a thin stream. Bring to a boil, whisking constantly. Cook for about 1 minute, whisking constantly. Reduce heat to low and return chicken to pot along with any accumulated juices.

Drop Dumpling batter by the tablespoonful onto the chicken in the pot. Continue until all batter is used. Cook uncovered for 10 minutes, then cover pot tightly and cook an additional 10 minutes. Serve immediately.

For the Dumplings:

Sift flour, baking powder and salt together in a medium bowl. Cut in the shortening until mixture resembles coarse meal. Stir in milk just until incorporated. Do not overmix.

Leslie J. Whipple

▪ SESAME BAKED CHICKEN ▪

3 3½-pound chickens, cut into serving pieces
2 cups buttermilk
1 cup melted butter
3 tablespoons lemon juice
½ teaspoon tarragon
4 cups fine bread crumbs
½ cup sesame seeds
¼ cup fresh parsley, minced
3 teaspoons seasoned salt

Preheat oven to 350 degrees.

Place chicken pieces in one layer in a shallow dish. Pour buttermilk over, cover tightly, and refrigerate overnight.

The next day, pour off buttermilk and pat chicken dry. Discard buttermilk. Combine melted butter, lemon juice and tarragon in a shallow dish. In another shallow dish, combine bread crumbs, sesame seeds, parsley and seasoned salt.

Dip chicken pieces in butter mixture then coat with crumb mixture. Arrange chicken in baking dish. Spoon remaining butter mixture over chicken. Cover with plastic wrap and refrigerate until 1½ hours before dinner.

Bake, without turning, for about 1½ hours, or until very tender. Baste occasionally with pan juices. To serve, arrange on a large platter and garnish with parsley and radish roses. Serves 12.

Dotti Wilson

▪ SWEET AND SOUR CHICKEN ▪

2 tablespoons vegetable oil
2½ pounds boneless chicken, cut into 2-inch pieces
¾ cup ketchup
½ cup brown sugar
⅓ cup vinegar
1 teaspoon mustard
2 16-ounce cans pineapple chunks and their juice
1 8-ounce can water chestnuts, sliced and drained

Heat oil in a large skillet over medium heat. Add chicken and brown on all sides. Drain off any fat. In a medium bowl stir together ketchup, brown sugar, vinegar and mustard until well blended. Stir into chicken in the skillet. Add pineapple and water chestnuts. Bring to a simmer then reduce heat to medium-low and simmer for 30 minutes. Serve with steamed white rice.

Barbara Curtis

What Ever Happened to the Foucault Pendulum?

The original OMSI building was centered around the Foucault Pendulum, which illustrated the rotation of the earth by its daily precession around a large circle of pegs set up on the museum's basement floor. The pendulum hung from a 60-foot wire that extended up into the building's clock tower. After the MGM fire in Las Vegas, the fire marshall's office was concerned that the column of air from the tower to the basement would create a chimney effect in the event of a fire. They ordered the hole through the first floor sealed, and the pendulum was removed.

▪ JOHN'S TERIYAKI CHICKEN ▪

½ cup soy sauce
½ cup sugar
¼ cup sake (Japanese rice wine)
2 cloves garlic, minced
½ teaspoon fresh ginger, grated
2 pounds boneless chicken, cut into 2-inch cubes

In a large skillet, combine soy sauce, sugar, sake, garlic and ginger. Bring to a boil over medium-high heat and boil until sugar dissolves and mixture has slightly thickened. Add chicken pieces, reduce heat to medium-low, and simmer for about 20 minutes, turning chicken every 5 minutes. Remove chicken and keep warm. Increase heat to medium-high and bring sauce to a boil. Boil until mixture has reduced to desired thickness. Pour glaze over chicken and serve with steamed rice and a light salad.

John L. Moore

▪ BERRY WINE GLAZE ▪

1 tablespoon sugar
1 tablespoon cornstarch
1 tablespoon cold water
½ cup berry wine (such as Kramer Vineyards' Raspberry, Blackberry or Boysenberry wine)
1 teaspoon vinegar
⅛ teaspoon cinnamon
⅛ teaspoon ginger

Combine sugar and cornstarch in a small sauce pan. Add water and stir to dissolve the mixture. Add berry wine. Place over medium heat and cook, whisking constantly, until slightly thickened. Add vinegar, cinnamon and ginger and continue cooking for one more minute.

Pour glaze over baked, roasted or poached chicken breast or a roasted Cornish game hen. Yum!

Trudy Kramer
Kramer Vineyards

▪ ROAST CHICKEN WITH ROSEMARY ▪

1 roasting chicken
4 cloves garlic, minced
2 tablespoons olive oil
1½ teaspoons dried rosemary, crushed with a mortar and pestle
1 teaspoon salt
Few grindings black pepper
1 small onion, quartered
1 stalk celery, cut into 1-inch pieces
Juice of 1 lemon
1½ cups dry white wine

Preheat oven to 350 degrees. Lightly oil a roasting pan.

Combine garlic, olive oil, rosemary, salt and pepper in a small bowl. Rub chicken inside and out with the mixture. Stuff cavity with the onion and celery, then truss. Roast the chicken for about 1 hour, or until done. Remove from oven and sprinkle all over with lemon juice. Remove chicken to a serving platter. Remove excess grease from pan. Place roasting pan on top of stove over medium-high heat. When hot, deglaze pan with wine and reduce by one-half, whisking constantly. Strain sauce and serve with chicken.

For a picnic, omit the white wine and deglazing the pan. Roast chicken according to the recipe and chill overnight.

Leslie J. Whipple

Why do chicken and turkeys have both light and dark meat? A substance called myoglobin, found in muscle cells, stores oxygen that is brought by the blood until it is used by the muscles during exercise. Muscles that are very active need more oxygen and have a higher concentration of myoglobin. Domesticated fowl stand, walk and run around so their legs are active and need more oxygen therefore the leg muscle is dark. Chicken and turkeys rarely fly so their breast muscles are light. Wild fowl fly and their breast muscle is as dark as their leg muscles.

▪ CHICKEN BREASTS WITH CHUTNEY AND MADEIRA ▪

3 whole chicken breasts; skinned, boned and split
3 tablespoons butter
2 green onions, including green tops, sliced
½ teaspoon fresh ginger, minced
3 tablespoons mango chutney, chopped
⅓ cup Madeira
¾ cup chicken stock
¾ cup heavy cream
Salt and pepper to taste
2 tablespoons crystallized ginger, minced

Melt butter in a large skillet over medium heat. Add chicken to skillet, without crowding, and cook until done, about 8 minutes per side. Remove to a platter and keep warm.

Add green onions, fresh ginger, chutney, Madeira and chicken stock to skillet. Increase heat to high and boil, whisking constantly, until reduced by half, about 4 minutes. Add cream and any accumulated juices from reserved chicken. Boil until slightly thickened. Season to taste with salt and pepper.

Spoon half the sauce over the chicken. Sprinkle with the crystallized ginger. Pass the remaining sauce. Serves 6.

Lynda Johnston

▪ LAST MINUTE COMPANY CHICKEN ▪

In a rush? Prepare a meal in 30 minutes that is fit for royalty.

Purchase 1 3-pound roasted chicken, cut in half*
12 whole mushrooms
1 green zucchini, sliced
2 tomatoes, cut in wedges
2 cups broccoli florets
2 cups cauliflower florets
1 bunch green onions, sliced
½ cup walnuts, chopped
1 teaspoon oregano
½ teaspoon pepper
Salt to taste
2 cups Swiss cheese, grated

Preheat oven to 350 degrees. Lightly oil a 9-inch by 13-inch glass baking dish.

Cut the roasted chicken in half length-wise and place in prepared baking dish skin-side up. Place in oven for 10 minutes. Remove from oven and smother chicken with vegetables. Sprinkle over walnuts, oregano, pepper and salt and return to the oven. Bake for 15 minutes or until vegetables are tender. Sprinkle grated cheese over the top and bake an additional 5 minutes or until melted and bubbly. Serve with crusty bread and enjoy!

*Or if you have time, cut a 3-pound chicken in half and place it in a glass baking dish, brush with 2 tablespoons margarine and sprinkle with salt, then roast at 350 degrees for 45 minutes.

Marilynne Eichinger

What's the difference between a crocodile and an alligator?

Alligators' snouts are rounded and the upper teeth are exposed when their mouths are closed. Crocodiles have a narrow snout and both upper and lower teeth are exposed when their mouths are closed. Crocodiles are more aggressive.

David Heil
Newton's Apple
Associate Director, OMSI

▪ RASPBERRY CHICKEN ▪

2 whole chicken breasts, halved
2 tablespoons flour
1½ tablespoons butter
1 tablespoon vegetable oil
¾ cup chicken stock
6 tablespoons raspberry vinegar
½ cup heavy cream
½ cup fresh raspberries

Lightly coat chicken breasts with flour. Melt butter and oil together in a skillet over medium heat. Brown chicken on both sides. Add chicken stock and vinegar to skillet and stir to deglaze pan. Reduce heat to low and simmer, uncovered, until chicken is done, about 25 minutes. Remove chicken to a plate and keep warm. Add cream to skillet and increase heat to medium-high. Cook, whisking often, until sauce has thickened enough to coat the back of a wooden spoon. Pour sauce over chicken and serve garnished with fresh raspberries. Serves 4.

Lisa Lemco

How does a crocodile hide in the water and still keep an eye on its prey?

A crocodile uses a principle of buoyancy to hide from it's prey. By swallowing stones, it can sink lower in the water, thus exposing less of itself.

David Heil
Newton's Apple
Associate Director, OMSI

▪ FRENCH POTTED CHICKEN ▪

This is a beautiful and tasty main dish that can be cooked and served in the same baking dish. The orange carrots and bright green peas with the chicken and potatoes makes it very appealing.

- ¼ cup flour
- 1 teaspoon salt
- ½ teaspoon paprika
- ¼ teaspoon black pepper, freshly ground
- 1 3 to 4-pound chicken, cut into serving pieces
- 2 tablespoons butter or margarine
- 1 cup water
- ½ teaspoon rosemary
- ¼ teaspoon marjoram
- 2 cups carrots, cut into julienne strips about 2-inches by ½-inch
- 1 cup water
- 1 10-ounce package frozen peas
- 1 12-ounce package frozen French-fried potatoes
- ½ teaspoon salt

Preheat oven to 400 degrees.

Combine flour, salt, paprika and pepper in a shallow dish, and stir to mix. Dredge chicken pieces well in flour mixture. Heat butter in an oven-proof Dutch oven on top of the stove. Brown the chicken on both sides.

Add 1 cup water, rosemary and marjoram, cover and bake in the oven for 35 minutes.

Add carrots, and 1 cup water. Return to the oven and bake for 20 minutes.

Add peas and French-fried potatoes, sprinkle with ½ teaspoon salt and bake an additional 15 minutes, uncovered, until heated through. Serves 6.

Carolyn Rose

▪ CHICKEN VERONA ▪

- 1 3-pound chicken, cut into serving pieces
- ½ cup olive oil
- 3 cloves garlic, minced
- 1 cup bread crumbs
- ⅓ cup Parmesan cheese, grated
- ¼ cup fresh parsley, minced
- 1 teaspoon salt
- ½ teaspoon dry mustard
- ¼ teaspoon black pepper

Preheat oven to 375 degrees. Lightly grease a shallow baking dish.

Combine olive oil and garlic in a bowl. Combine bread crumbs, Parmesan cheese, parsley, salt, dry mustard and pepper in a separate bowl. Dip chicken pieces first in oil mixture, then dredge in crumb mixture. Place chicken pieces in prepared baking dish and bake about 45 minutes, or until brown and crispy.

Sylvia Gere Emard

"The most beautiful experience we can have is the mysterious. It is the fundamental emotion which stands at the cradle of true arts and science."

—Albert Einstein,
as quoted by Geordi LaForge,
from the Kendall Planetarium show
Orion Rendezvous: A "Star Trek" Voyage of Discovery

Mark Bourne

▪ MARYLAND FRIED CHICKEN ▪

1 frying chicken, cut into serving pieces
⅓ cup flour
1 teaspoon salt
¼ teaspoon black pepper
¼ cup water
1 egg
2 cups fresh bread crumbs
⅓ cup oil for frying

Preheat oven to 350 degrees.

In a shallow bowl, mix together flour, salt and pepper. In a separate shallow bowl whisk together water and egg until smooth. Place bread crumbs in a third shallow bowl. Dredge chicken pieces in flour mixture. Then dip in egg mixture. Then coat with bread crumbs.

Heat oil in a skillet over medium heat. Brown prepared chicken pieces on all sides. Remove and place chicken in a shallow baking dish. Sprinkle with 1 tablespoon water and any remaining bread crumbs. Cover baking dish tightly and bake for 1 hour. Yum!

Joy Renick (Mrs. Terry)

▪ MORIN'S LANDING'S SWEET AND SOUR CHOKE CHERRY GLAZE ▪

This glaze is ideal for chicken, pork, beef or fish. It can also be used for barbecuing.

10 ounces Morin's Landing Choke Cherry Jam
¼ cup red wine vinegar
2 tablespoons Worcestershire sauce
1 tablespoon soy sauce
2 tablespoons cornstarch
½ cup water

In a medium sauce pan, combine Choke Cherry Jam, vinegar, Worcestershire sauce and soy sauce. Dissolve cornstarch in water and add to mixture. Bring mixture to a boil, and boil for 3 minutes, whisking constantly.

Joyce Bolliger
Morin's Landing

▪ DAVE'S "HAVE A BEER" CHILI ▪

1 tablespoon vegetable oil
2 pounds ground turkey
2 medium onions, chopped
1 green bell pepper, seeded and chopped
4 cloves garlic, minced
1 bunch cilantro, minced
1 32-ounce can Cajun-style tomatoes
1 Full Sail Amber Beer
2 tablespoons chili powder
1½ tablespoons cumin
2 teaspoons salt
1½ teaspoons black pepper
1 28-ounce can kidney beans, drain and reserve half of the liquid

In a large pot, heat oil and brown turkey over medium heat. Drain off fat and add onions, green pepper, garlic and cilantro and sauté until tender. Add tomatoes, beer, chili powder, cumin, salt and pepper then reduce heat to low and simmer, partially covered, for 1 hour. Stir occasionally and add water if it gets too dry. Stir in beans and half of their liquid and simmer over low heat for 20 minutes. Serve with good Italian Bread.

Bradley Cook

▪ FRUITED CHICKEN BREASTS ▪

3 tablespoons flour
1 teaspoon paprika
1 to 2 tablespoons olive oil
2 whole chicken breasts; halved, skinned and boned
⅓ cup apricot preserves
1 16-ounce can apricot halves **OR** sliced peaches in natural juice
1 tablespoon fresh lemon juice
1 tablespoon dry sherry
2 teaspoons soy sauce
1½ teaspoons brown sugar
¼ teaspoon Chinese chili paste
¼ cup sliced almonds, toasted
2 green onions, including the green part, sliced

Preheat oven to 350 degrees. Lightly oil an 8-inch by 8-inch baking dish with a non-stick spray.

Combine flour and paprika in a shallow dish. Heat oil in a large, non-stick skillet over medium heat. Dredge chicken breasts in flour mixture and place in skillet. Brown on both sides. Arrange browned breasts in prepared baking dish and spread evenly with apricot preserves.

Drain canned apricots, pouring juice into a medium bowl and reserving apricots. Stir lemon juice, sherry, soy sauce, brown sugar and chili paste into the apricot juice. Pour mixture over chicken and cover tightly with foil. Bake for 30 minutes. Remove foil and bake an additional 10 minutes. Add reserved apricots and bake an additional 5 minutes, or until apricots are heated through.

Serve garnished with almonds and green onions. Serves 4.

Jim and Karen Bosley

To remember the planets and their order, use this saying:

Mankind's **V**erdent **E**arth **M**ust **J**ourney
as a
Star **U**nites **N**ine **P**lanets.

Planets in Order From the Sun:

Planet # 1	Mercury	Mankind's
Planet # 2	Venus	Verdent
Planet # 3	Earth	Earth
Planet # 4	Mars	Must
Planet # 5	Jupiter	Journey
		as a
Planet # 6	Saturn	Star
Planet # 7	Uranus	Unites
Planet # 8	Neptune	Nine
Planet # 9	Pluto	Planets

JOHN FOSTER

▪ SPRING STEW OF OREGON CHICKEN AND RABBIT ▪

WITH MOREL MUSHROOMS, ASPARAGUS AND TARRAGON

2 tablespoons olive oil
1 rabbit, skinned and boned and cut into 2-inch pieces
2 chicken breasts, skinned and boned and cut into 2-inch pieces
¼ pound morel mushrooms, washed and dried
2 tomatoes; peeled, seeded and chopped
8 cloves garlic, peeled and poached until tender
Salt and white pepper to taste
½ cup dry white wine
2 cups white stock **OR** chicken stock
2 tablespoons arrowroot
¼ pound asparagus, cut into 1-inch pieces and blanched
¼ cup fresh tarragon, chopped
4-inch by 4-inch puff pastry shells

In a large Dutch oven or skillet, heat oil over medium heat and sauté the rabbit and chicken until evenly browned. Add the morel mushrooms and continue to sauté until tender. Add tomatoes and garlic. Season with salt and white pepper. Increase the heat to medium-high and stir in the white wine. Dissolve the arrowroot in the white stock and add to stew. Reduce heat to medium and bring to a simmer, allowing the sauce to clear and thicken. Add the asparagus and tarragon and heat through.

Place puff pastry shells on serving plates and spoon the stew into and around the pastry. Spoon sauce over all and serve immediately. Serves 4.

Mark Altstetter
The Heathman Hotel
Portland, Oregon

MEATS

▪ Camp Kiwanilong ▪

OMSI uses the Clatsop County-owned Camp Kiwanilong for it's coastal programs spring and fall for schools and other groups and during the summer for camp sessions. Located on the northern Oregon coast 12 miles from Seaside, this camp is within walking distance of the ocean. The facility borders Long Lake, a protected area for canoeing, fishing, and swimming. A beautiful log cabin lodge has a modern kitchen and dining hall where meals are served family style for up to 80 people. Lights out is no problem in the 10 rustic cabins. There is no electricity so when the flashlights go out, it's bedtime. The cabins sleep eight people who bring sleeping bags and pads. Although the sleeping accommodations are rustic, the restrooms have electricity and hot and cold running water. An infirmary, and a laboratory and nature center complete the camp.

Campers at the Pacific Marine Science camps investigate tide pools, how sand dunes are formed and how humans manipulate them, the adaptations of coastal plants and animals, the role estuaries play in coastal ecology, currents and tides, the complexities of the Columbia River bar, and the coastal forests.

Of course as at any camp, crafts, recreation and evening campfires round out the scientific learning that takes place.

Connie Hofferber Jones

▪ GRILLED BEEF TENDERLOIN MARINATED IN PINOT NOIR, GARLIC AND ROSEMARY ▪

Choose Montinore's Pinot Noir for a special occasion and enjoy it with someone you love. This recipe is conceived especially for our pinot noir. The wine's spicy style will not diminish while using the garlic and rosemary which add a subtle sparkle to the finish of the wine. When you choose pinot noir, you also choose an elegant menu for entertaining.

1 whole beef tenderloin, 3 to 4 pounds, tail and head secured with kitchen twine

Marinade:

2 cups extra virgin olive oil
1 cup Montinore Pinot Noir
½ medium red onion, sliced
3 shallots, minced
3 cloves garlic, minced
2 bay leaves, crumbled
1 tablespoon freshly cracked black peppercorns
2 sprigs fresh rosemary, crumbled (or 1½ tablespoons dried rosemary leaves)

Place beef in a glass or ceramic dish. Whisk together marinade ingredients and pour over meat. Cover with plastic wrap and refrigerate overnight, turning 2 to 3 times.

Heat charcoal in barbecue, or smoker to high, with grill at least 3-inches from heat. Remove meat from marinade and strain marinade. Pat meat dry with paper towels and let warm to room temperature before grilling.

Place meat on grill and cook for 30 minutes, basting with marinade, turning to sear on all sides. Do not overcook.

Remove from grill, remove string and let stand for 10 minutes. Slice across grain and drizzle with 1 teaspoon of extra virgin olive oil if desired. Serves 4 to 6.

Kenneth and Carol Hicks
Montinore Vineyards

▪ SHIP WRECK STEW ▪

2 tablespoons vegetable oil
¾ cup onion, sliced
3 cups potatoes, peeled and diced
1 pound hamburger
¼ cup uncooked rice
1 cup celery, sliced
2 cups cooked kidney beans
1 cup tomato sauce
½ cup water
½ teaspoon salt
½ teaspoon chili powder
¼ teaspoon Worcestershire sauce

Put oil in the bottom of a large Dutch oven or pot with a tight-fitting lid. Layer ingredients starting with onions, then potatoes, hamburger, rice, celery and kidney beans. In a small bowl, stir together tomato sauce, water, salt, chili powder and Worcestershire sauce. Pour over ingredients in pot. Cover tightly and bring to a boil. Reduce heat to low and simmer, covered for about 1½ hours.

Dotti Wilson

▪ CHILE CON CARNE ▪

1½ pounds beef stew meat, diced
1 tablespoon olive oil
2 medium onions, chopped
1 small green pepper, chopped
1 clove garlic, minced
2 jalepeno peppers, seeded and minced
1 to 1½ tablespoons chili powder
½ teaspoon dried, crushed red pepper
½ teaspoon salt
¼ teaspoon oregano
2½ cups water
1 12-ounce can tomato paste
1 15-ounce can pinto beans, drained

In a large Dutch oven or pot, heat olive oil over medium heat. Add the beef and brown on all sides. Add onions, green pepper and garlic and cook until onions are translucent. Stir in chili powder, dried red pepper, salt and oregano. Add water and tomato paste and stir until well blended. Increase heat and bring to a boil, stirring often. Reduce heat to low and simmer, uncovered, for 1½ hours, stirring occasionally. Stir in beans, cover pot, and simmer an additional 30 minutes. Serves 8.

Peter DeFazio
Member of Congress

▪ FLANK STEAK TACOS ▪

This is delicious hot or cold.

1½ pounds flank steak, cut into 1-inch cubes
½ cup white wine vinegar
3 tablespoons Italian seasoning
2 cloves garlic, minced

Accompaniments:
Flour tortillas
Tomatoes, chopped
Onions, chopped
Sour cream

In a 2-quart pot, put the flank steak, vinegar, Italian seasoning, garlic and add just enough water to cover the meat. Bring to a boil, then reduce heat to medium-low and simmer until the liquid is gone. Add enough water to cover meat again, and simmer over medium-low heat, until liquid is gone.

Using two forks, shred meat. Serve with flour tortillas and desired accompaniments.

Rita Adams

▪ CHILI CON ARROZ ▪

I've made this chili for years, to wide audiences who have happily gobbled it down.

1 to 2 tablespoons vegetable oil
2 to 3 large onions, sliced and quartered
2 cloves garlic, minced
1 green pepper, seeded and chopped
2 tablespoons chili powder
1½ teaspoons cumin
4 whole cloves
1 bay leaf, broken
1 pound ground sirloin
1 1-pound can peeled tomatoes
1 8-ounce can tomato sauce
2 15-ounce cans red kidney beans, including the liquid (I use low-salt)
1 15-ounce can garbanzo beans, drained
1 cup water
Salt to taste, if desired
Brown rice, cooked
Cheddar cheese
Plain yogurt

In a large pot, heat oil over medium heat. Add onions and garlic and sauté until translucent. Add green pepper, chili powder, cumin, cloves and bay leaf and cook for 2 minutes stirring constantly. Add meat and cook, stirring to break up, until no longer pink. Drain off any grease. Add tomatoes, tomato sauce, kidney beans, garbanzo beans, water and salt if desired. Bring to a boil then reduce heat to low and simmer, covered, for about 40 minutes. Uncover and simmer until desired thickness.

Serve in large bowls over brown rice, topped with grated cheese and a dollop of yogurt. I serve it with carrot sticks and saltine crackers on the side. Serves about 6.

Janet Filips

▪ MARVELOUS MEATLOAF FOR MUSEUM MEMBERS (AND OTHERS) ▪

I come from a family of scientists. My uncle, "Goody" Gregory Pincus, was the co-inventor of the birth control pill. These were known to many as "Pincus Pills for Prolific People"!

1 pound lean ground beef
1 pound ground veal
½ pound mild Italian sausage, removed from casings and crumbled
1 10-ounce package frozen spinach, thawed and squeezed dry
1 medium onion, minced
2 eggs, beaten
1 cup fresh bread crumbs
½ cup fresh Parmesan cheese, grated
¼ cup milk
1 tablespoon salt
½ teaspoon basil
½ teaspoon nutmeg
½ teaspoon thyme
1 10-ounce package frozen tiny green peas, thawed
½ cup pine nuts

Preheat oven to 350 degrees.

In a large bowl, combine the beef, veal, sausage, drained spinach, onion, eggs, bread crumbs, Parmesan, milk, salt, basil, nutmeg and thyme. Mix gently with hands until just blended. Gently fold in peas and pine nuts. Do not overmix.

Divide mixture in half and gently form into 2 10-inch long loaves. Place loaves on a 15-inch by 10-inch by 1-inch jelly roll pan. Bake for 1½ hours, basting often with pan juices. Remove from oven and cool in the pan. Baste with pan juices to glaze.

When cool, wrap each loaf in foil and refrigerate overnight. Let warm slightly before serving. This is perfect for a buffet or picnic. Serves 16 to 20.

Judy Amster

▪ BEEF STEW ▪

2 pounds stew beef, cut into 1½-inch cubes
¼ cup flour
1½ teaspoons salt
½ teaspoon pepper
3 tablespoons olive oil
4 cups tomato and vegetable juice, like V-8 Juice **OR** 4 cups tomato juice
4 bay leaves
2 tablespoons fresh parsley, minced
2 to 3 cloves garlic, minced
1 teaspoon oregano
1 teaspoon thyme
6 medium carrots, peeled and quartered
3 parsnips, peeled and quartered
2 potatoes, peeled and quartered
2 turnips, peeled and quartered
2 medium onions, quartered

Preheat oven to 350 degrees.

Combine flour, salt and pepper in a bowl and dredge beef lightly in mixture. Heat oil in a large Dutch oven or pot over medium heat. Add meat, one layer at a time, and brown meat well on all sides. Remove browned meat and set aside until all meat is browned. Whisk remaining flour into oil in pot then slowly whisk in tomato juice. Return meat to pot. Stir in bay leaves, parsley, garlic, oregano and thyme. Cover tightly and place in oven for 1½ hours. Add water to pot if mixture gets dry. Stir in vegetables, cover and bake an additional 1 hour, or until vegetables are tender.

Serve with a green salad and bread. Whoever gets a bay leaf in their bowl gets to make a wish on it!

Marcia Johnson Whipple

▪ Traveling Light ▪

Space travelers are always concerned about weight. Because of the gravitational attraction between a spacecraft and the Earth, it takes a large amount of energy to reach space. The lighter a spacecraft, the less energy it takes for a flight which makes for a less expensive mission.

All planning for space flight incorporates the need for weight conservation, including meal planning. NASA has developed some ingenious ways of providing food and drink for astronauts while conserving weight. One fascinating example is the way in which astronauts obtain their drinking water.

Aboard the space shuttle electricity is produced by a device called a fuel cell. Inside the fuel cell a chemical reaction takes place where hydrogen, H_2, is combined with oxygen, O_2, creating energy. The chemical by-product of the reaction is water, H_2O. It is water produced by the fuel cell that provides the shuttle crew with drinking water. In fact the fuel cell produces so much water that excess is released into space where it immediately freezes and then sublimes, or evaporates, like dry ice. Water from the fuel cell does away with the need for stored water aboard the shuttle and thus saves weight.

Freeze dried foods are another way space travelers save weight. With all water removed, freeze dried foods are very light. Because they are light, they are inexpensive, relatively speaking, to launch into space. Once in space, they are rehydrated using fuel cell water to provide astronauts with a meal. Energy and money are saved by removing water, and thus weight, from the food before leaving the ground.

Rob Grover

▪ SUBMARINE SHISH KEBAB ▪

This recipe was contrived and served to the Chief Petty Officers aboard the USS Blueback in the summer of 1981.

Marinade:

5 cups water
2½ cups soy sauce
1 cup cooking wine **OR** dry sherry
¼ cup sugar
1 teaspoon garlic, minced
1 teaspoon fresh ginger, minced
4 bay leaves
10 pounds tenderloin sheath, or other tender cut of beef
5 green bell peppers, cut into strips
3 pints cherry tomatoes
3 pints mushrooms
3 bunches green onions, cut into thirds

For the Marinade:

Combine marinade ingredients in a sauce pan and bring to a boil. Reduce heat to low and simmer for 15 minutes. Let cool completely.

Trim the beef well. Cut tenderloin into 1-inch cubes and place in a large bowl. Pour marinade over and stir to coat well. Cover and refrigerate for 24 hours, stirring occasionally to distribute marinade.

Prepare the vegetables. Alternate meat and vegetables on skewers. The tomatoes should not be last since they tend to get mushy and fall off. Grill over a charcoal fire, turning to cook on all sides until done, about 20 to 30 minutes.

Charlie Vanden Heuvel

▪ PRODUCE ROW'S RED EYE CHILI ▪

3½ pounds ground beef
3 onions, chopped
3 #10 cans (5½ pounds) kidney beans, (about 16 pounds total kidney beans)
3 #10 cans (5½ pounds) tomato sauce, (about 16 pounds total tomato sauce)
5 tablespoons chili powder
3½ tablespoons red pepper flakes
3 tablespoons garlic salt
1 tablespoon black pepper
Tabasco sauce to taste

In a very large pot, brown the beef. Add onions and sauté until tender. Drain off fat. Add kidney beans and tomato sauce. Add remaining ingredients and bring to a boil. Reduce heat to low and simmer, uncovered, for about 1 hour. Makes about 5 gallons and serves 50.

David West
Produce Row Cafe
Portland, Oregon

▪ TAMALE JOE CASSEROLE ▪

½ pound link sausage, sliced
1½ pounds ground beef
1 large onion, chopped
1 12-ounce can corn, drained
2 8-ounce cans tomato sauce
1 cup milk
1 tablespoon chili powder
2 teaspoons salt
¼ teaspoon black pepper
½ cup cornmeal
1 3½-ounce can ripe pitted olives, drained and sliced
1 cup cheddar cheese, grated

Preheat oven to 325 degrees. Lightly grease a 9-inch by 13-inch baking dish.

In a large skillet, brown sausage over medium heat. Pour off fat. Add ground beef, onion and corn and sauté until meat is cooked and onion is tender. Add tomato sauce, milk, chili powder, salt and pepper and stir to blend. Reduce heat to low and simmer for 20 minutes. Stir cornmeal into meat mixture. Stir in olives. Pour into prepared baking dish and sprinkle cheese on top. Bake for 40 minutes. Serves 6 to 8.

Terry Hiller

▪ TAMALE PIE ▪

This recipe can be multiplied for a crowd. Following are recipes to serve 8 and to serve 50.

For 8 Servings:

1½ pounds ground beef
1 cup onion, chopped
½ cup green bell pepper, chopped
1 clove garlic, minced
2½ cups canned tomatoes
1 12-ounce can whole kernel corn
1½ tablespoons chili powder
1½ teaspoons salt
¼ teaspoon black pepper
½ cup cornmeal
1 cup water
1 cup ripe pitted olives, chopped

Topping for 8 Servings:

1½ cups milk
2 tablespoons butter
1 teaspoon salt
½ cup cornmeal
2 eggs, beaten
1 cup grated Cheddar **OR** Monterey Jack cheese

For 50 Servings:

9 pounds ground beef
6 cups onion, chopped
3 cups green bell pepper, chopped
6 cloves garlic, minced
1 #10 can (1 gallon) canned tomatoes
72-ounces canned whole kernel corn
¾ cup chili powder
3 tablespoons salt
2 teaspoons black pepper
3 cups cornmeal
6 cups water
6 cups ripe pitted olives, chopped

Topping for 50 Servings:

9 cups milk
¾ cup butter
1 tablespoon salt
3 cups cornmeal
12 eggs, beaten
6 cups grated Cheddar **OR** Monterey Jack cheese

Preheat oven to 350 degrees. Lightly oil one **OR** six 9-inch by 13-inch baking pans.

In a large skillet, brown the meat over medium heat. Add onion, green pepper and garlic and cook until onion is golden. Stir in tomatoes, corn, chili powder, salt and pepper. Simmer for 5 minutes. Stir cornmeal and water together then add to meat mixture. Stir well. Add olives. Pour mixture into prepared pan.

For the Topping:

In a large sauce pan, heat milk, butter and salt over low heat. Slowly stir in cornmeal. Cook, stirring constantly, until thick. Remove from heat and stir in eggs and cheese. Pour over meat mixture in pan.

Bake for 40 minutes or until hot and bubbly around the edges.

Connie Hofferber Jones

▪ BARBECUED TOP ROUND STEAK ▪

1½ pounds top round steak

Marinade:

¼ cup vegetable oil
2 tablespoons soy sauce
1 tablespoon cider vinegar
2 teaspoons honey
1½ teaspoons garlic powder
1 teaspoon ground ginger
3 green onions, chopped

Combine all marinade ingredients and stir well. Score meat lightly and place in marinade. Marinate at least 4 hours or overnight, turning occasionally. Remove meat from marinade and reserve marinade. Grill meat over medium coals, brushing meat with reserved marinade often. Serves 4 to 6.

Toni J. Ives

▪ SPRING LAMB SHANK STEW ▪

5 pounds lamb shanks
3 cloves garlic, cut into thick slivers
½ cup olive oil
1 teaspoon oregano
1 teaspoon rosemary
Salt and pepper to taste
1½ cups chicken broth
1 cup water
1 cup dry white wine
Juice and rind of 1 lemon
6 carrots, cut into 2-inch pieces
4 large potatoes, peeled and quartered
1 10-ounce package frozen peas, thawed and drained
1 10-ounce package frozen string beans, thawed and drained

Preheat oven to 400 degrees.

Pierce the lamb shanks with a small, sharp knife and stud with the slivers of garlic. Place lamb in a Dutch oven or heavy pot and sprinkle with olive oil, oregano, rosemary, salt and pepper. Place in oven and roast for 30 minutes. Lower temperature to 325 and add chicken broth, water, wine, lemon juice and rind. Cover and bake for 1½ hours. Add carrots and potatoes. Cover and bake an additional hour. Add peas and string beans and bake an additional 15 minutes or until done. Serve over rice.

Senator and Mrs. Mark O. Hatfield

"Cadets, you'd better be ready to experience more wonders than you've ever imagined. Thanks to the science and scientists who came before us, especially the pioneers of the 20th and 21st centuries, the Universe is opening it's secrets to humanity. There are marvels and mysteries out there that will keep scientists at work for centuries."

—Geordi LaForge
(played by LeVar Burton)
from the Kendall Planetarium
show Orion Rendezvous:
A "Star Trek" Voyage of Discovery

Mark Bourne

▪ LEG OF LAMB IN SAUERKRAUT ▪

2 pounds Steinfeld's Sauerkraut
Boiling water
¼ cup olive oil
2 bay leaves
Freshly ground pepper
Leg of lamb
1 cup chicken broth
¼ pound pitted Greek olives
1 cup sour cream

Preheat oven to 350 degrees.

Drain sauerkraut and pour boiling water over it. Drain well. Put sauerkraut in heavy saucepan with olive oil, crumbled bay leaves and pepper. Cover and cook over low heat for about 1 hour, or until golden brown.

Put lamb in a roasting pan with chicken broth. Cover the meat with the sauerkraut mixture and add Greek olives. Cover tightly and bake for about 1¾ hours. Stir in sour cream. Cover pan and bake an additional 15 minutes.

Serve with small, boiled red potatoes. Serves 6 to 8.

Ray Steinfeld, Jr.
Steinfeld's
Products
Company

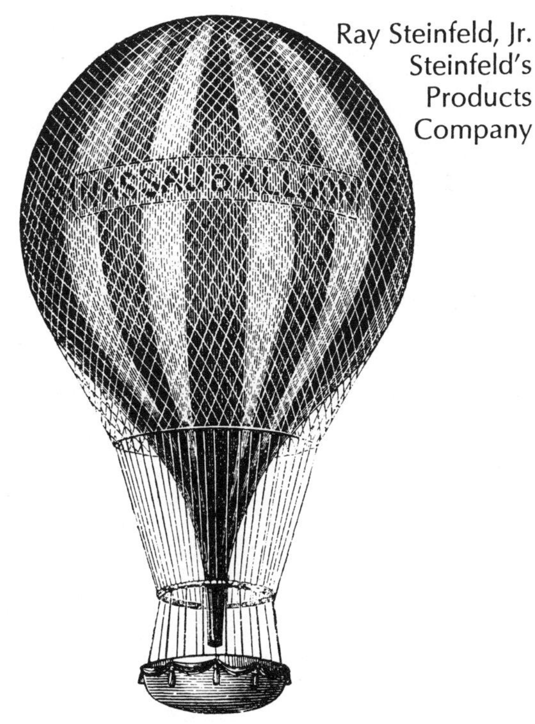

▪ TUMBET ▪

For many years, one of my deer hunting companions in Eastern Oregon was Bill Cifre who had been born and spent his boyhood in Majorca, Spain as a sheepherder. He used to prepare a meal for our hunting club that the shepherds made with lamb, eggplant, potatoes, tomatoes, green onions and various seasonings. The meal was assembled in a Dutch oven that was buried in the coals of the fire in the morning and was ready to serve when the tired sheepherders returned late in the day. It was called "Tumbet." In his later years, Bill developed this simplified version of the recipe that I find quite satisfying.

3 to 4 pounds lamb blade chops
2 eggplants
2 eggs
1/4 cup milk
2 bunches green onions including the green part, chopped
2 14-ounce cans tomato sauce
1 14-ounce bag potato chips
Black pepper to taste

Preheat oven to 325 degrees.

Place the lamb in a large pot and add enough water to come halfway up the sides of the meat. Cover and braise until the lamb is very tender and the bones come out easily, about 1 hour. While the lamb is cooking, prepare the eggplant. Slice eggplant 1/2-inch thick. Beat eggs and milk together until well blended. Dip eggplant slices in egg mixture and place on lightly greased baking sheets. Broil on both sides until nicely browned.

Put half of the eggplant in the bottom of a Dutch oven or heavy casserole then layer with half of the cooked lamb, half of the potato chips, half of the green onions, and pour over 1 can of tomato sauce. Repeat with remaining ingredients. Sprinkle with pepper. Cover and bake at 325 degrees for about 3 hours.

Serve with a simple salad and French bread. The left-overs are delicious reheated.

Jean W. Scheel

▪ PORK FILET WITH HONEY AND GINGER AND PINEAPPLE SALSA ▪

2 pounds pork tenderloin
1/4 cup rice wine vinegar
2 tablespoons olive oil
2 cloves garlic, minced
2 teaspoons honey
1 teaspoon fresh ginger, grated
1 teaspoon fish sauce (also called nuac mam in Asian grocery stores)
Freshly ground black pepper to taste
Pineapple Salsa, recipe below

Remove all visible fat from meat and place in a shallow glass dish. In a small bowl, combine vinegar, oil, garlic, honey, ginger, fish sauce and pepper. Pour over meat and turn to coat all sides. Cover and refrigerate at least 2 hours or overnight.

Broil or grill on barbecue until internal temperature reaches 150 degrees. Meat will be slightly pink inside. Allow pork to sit for 5 minutes before slicing. Carve into 1/2-inch slices and serve with Pineapple Salsa. Serves 4.

Pineapple Salsa

2 cups fresh pineapple (about 1/2 of a pineapple), diced
1/4 cup sweet red bell pepper, finely diced
Juice of 1/2 lime
1 tablespoon fresh cilantro, minced
2 teaspoons honey
1 teaspoon fresh ginger, grated

Combine all ingredients in a medium bowl. Refrigerate, covered, in a glass or other non-reactive container, for at least 2 hours to allow flavors to marry. Serve at room temperature. Makes about 2 1/2 cups.

Jim and Karen Bosley

Citrus fruits are native to Southeast Asia. Lemons, oranges and limes were cultivated in China, India and Japan. Grapefruit are a recent hybrid of the orange and pummelo.

▪ PORK ROAST SMOTHERED IN KRAUT ▪

2 to 3 pounds lean pork roast **OR** 2 to 3 pounds boneless spareribs
Flour
1 pint sauerkraut, fresh or from a glass jar
White wine **OR** apple juice
2 tablespoons brown sugar
1 teaspoon whole caraway seeds
1 apple; peeled, cored and quartered (optional)

Preheat oven to 350 degrees.

Dredge pork in unseasoned flour, shaking off the excess. Place pork, fatter side up, in a large, oven-proof Dutch oven or heavy pot that has a lid. Place in the oven, uncovered, and roast until well browned, about 1 hour. Remove from oven and drain off all fat.

Drain the sauerkraut into a container. Measure liquid, then discard. Replace sauerkraut liquid with an equal amount of wine OR apple juice. Smother pork with sauerkraut, wine, brown sugar, caraway and apple. Cover pot with a tight-fitting lid and return to oven. Continue cooking until meat is tender, about 1 additional hour. Serve with boiled potatoes and a green salad.

John L. Moore

▪ OLD WEST COWBOY PORK CHOPS ▪

6 pork chops, ¾-inch thick
4 tablespoons vegetable oil
2 medium onions, sliced
2 teaspoons chili powder
1 green bell pepper, chopped
1 cup uncooked rice
2 8-ounce cans tomato sauce
1¼ cups water
2 teaspoons salt

Preheat oven to 375 degrees.

Heat the oil in a large skillet over medium heat. Add the pork chops and brown well on both sides. Remove pork and set aside. Add onions and sauté until lightly browned. Remove onions and set aside. Add chili powder to pan and cook, stirring, for 2 minutes. Add green pepper, rice, tomato sauce, water and salt to skillet and stir until well blended. Bring to a boil.

Pour tomato mixture into an 8-cup shallow baking pan. Arrange pork chops in the mixture and place the onions between them. Cover pan with foil and place in oven. Bake for 1 hour or until liquid is absorbed by the rice. Serves 6.

Charlene Perkins

So, just how much DNA is there in our body, anyway?

If the nearly six feet of DNA in each of your cells were spread out end to end, the chain would reach more than eleven billion miles. I'd say that's plenty, wouldn't you!

David Heil
Newton's Apple
Associate Director, OMSI

▪ PORK CHOPS BALSAMICA ▪

2 tablespoons butter
4 thick pork chops
½ cup Balsamic vinegar
½ cup chicken stock **OR** water
2 tablespoons cold butter, cut into small pieces

Heat 2 tablespoons butter in a large skillet over medium heat. Add pork chops and brown well on both sides. Reduce heat to low and cook until done. Remove pork chops and keep warm.

Pour off excess fat from skillet. Whisk in vinegar and stock and reduce by half. Reduce heat to low. Add 2 tablespoons cold butter a little at a time, whisking constantly to emulsify butter with each addition, until all butter is used. Pour sauce over pork chops and serve immediately. Serves 4.

Leo MacLeod

▪ TIGER CHOW ▪

Now I know this dish may not sound like a gourmet meal, but it is intended as a dinner to eat while camping, and as such, is delicious. This dish was inspired by necessity while I was trekking in the wilds of Tasmania searching for the Tasmanian Tiger. I needed a hearty meal whose ingredients could last up to three weeks without refrigeration. After a little experimentation, I came up with a tasty stew that we called Tiger Chow. We enjoyed this meal almost every other day and never grew tired of it.

2 potatoes, cut into 1-inch cubes
1 medium carrot, diced
1 stalk celery, diced
¼ cup butter
¼ pound spicy Italian sausage, sliced
1 medium onion, chopped
1 clove garlic, minced
Salt and pepper to taste

Place cubed potatoes in a large pot and barely cover with water. Simmer over medium-low heat until halfway done. Throw in diced carrot. A few minutes later, throw in the celery. Season with salt and pepper.

Heat butter in a large skillet and sauté sausage, onion and garlic until meat is cooked and onion is transparent. When potatoes are almost done, mix in the sausage mixture and stir to combine. Cook together for about 5 minutes to allow flavors to blend, stirring often. The potatoes will make a thick stock for the stew, and still leave big, bite-sized pieces to enjoy.

Steve Robertson

▪ SWEET AND HOT MUSTARD ▪

6 eggs
1 4-ounce can Colman's Dry Mustard
1 cup sugar
1 cup rice vinegar

In a medium bowl, beat eggs until light and foamy. Add mustard, sugar and vinegar and blend until smooth. Transfer mixture to the top of a double-boiler. Cook over simmering water, whisking constantly until thick and smooth. Store in the refrigerator. Makes about 1 quart. Serve with ham.

Claris Poppert

▪ POTAWATOMI STUFFED SUGAR PUMPKIN ▪

The Prairie Band of the Potawatomi Tribe are one of the many Plains tribes that had it's origin in the Great Lakes and in the northern woodlands. Thus they were familiar with wild rice. It became an important trade item, finding it's way from Woodland to Prairie tribes. It was traded for buffalo hides and dried meats from the hunting peoples on the Plains, who were long removed from their ancestral rice marshes.

1 4-pound to 5-pound sugar pumpkin
1 teaspoon salt
½ teaspoon dry mustard
1 to 2 tablespoons vegetable oil **OR** rendered fat
1 pound ground venison **OR** buffalo **OR** beef
1 medium onion, chopped
1 cup cooked wild rice
3 eggs, beaten
1 teaspoon sage
1 teaspoon salt
¼ teaspoon black pepper

Preheat oven to 350 degrees.

Cut the top off the pumpkin and remove seeds and strings. Prick cavity of the pumpkin all over with a fork. Combine 1 teaspoon salt with dry mustard and rub the cavity.

Heat oil in a large skillet over medium-high heat. Add meat and onion and sauté until browned. Remove pan off the heat and stir in wild rice, eggs, sage, 1 teaspoon salt and pepper. Blend well and stuff mixture into pumpkin.

Put pumpkin in a shallow baking dish and add enough water to come up ½-inch. Bake for 1½ hours, or until pumpkin is very tender. Add more water to the pan as necessary to avoid sticking. Cut pumpkin into wedges, giving each person both pumpkin and stuffing. Serves 6.

Michael Ray

▪ ORIENTAL MARINADE ▪

This is a delicious marinade for beef or chicken.

1 cup salad oil
1 cup low-sodium soy sauce
¼ cup rice vinegar
½ cup onion, chopped
¼ cup candied ginger, chopped
3 cloves garlic, minced
½ teaspoon dry mustard
½ teaspoon black pepper

Combine all ingredients and whisk until blended. Depending on the variety and cut of meat, marinate for as little as 1 hour, (for boneless chicken breasts), to overnight, (for flank steak). Baste meat with marinade while cooking for stronger flavor. Makes about 3 cups.

Claris Poppert

▪ LEO'S BARBEQUE SAUCE ▪

¼ cup vegetable oil
1 large onion, chopped
4 cloves garlic, minced
1½ cups ketchup
1 6-ounce can tomato paste
½ cup cider vinegar
½ cup water
2 tablespoons Dijon mustard
2 tablespoons molasses
1 tablespoon horseradish
1 tablespoon brown sugar
1 tablespoon Worcestershire sauce
½ teaspoon chili powder
½ teaspoon Tabasco sauce

Heat oil in a large pot over medium heat. Add onion and garlic and sauté until tender. Add remaining ingredients and stir to blend well. Bring to a boil, then reduce heat to low and simmer for about 40 minutes. Makes enough Leo's Barbeque Sauce for 15 ribs with extra sauce.

Leo MacLeod

BREADS

▪ Science Programs ▪

OMSI was founded on the principle of participatory science education. Ever since the museum's beginnings, a host of science programs behind the scenes have given students, teachers and families the opportunity to capture the OMSI experience outside the museum. OMSI's traveling science programs go where no museum has gone before, treating students from Oregon and, currently, six other states to adventures in science right in their own schools! As a result, hundreds of thousands of youngsters in areas far from Portland have performed experiments using lasers, explored the insides of a squid, traveled through the night sky in a portable planetarium, and much more. In-house classes are also packed year-round with kids probing such subjects as chemistry, astronomy, and environmental science.

Special programs aren't limited to students: their teachers can also take advantage of OMSI's workshops and classes, and for the truly ambitious, OMSI offers graduate courses in science and math education in cooperation with Lewis and Clark and Portland State Universities. The OMSI Education Resource Center in Washington Park now provides more room for these in-house programs, and next year the museum hopes to offer a fifth-year pre-certification program focused on science education.

Here in the city, OMSI's Alberta Science Center for Kids (better known as A.S.K.-OMSI) continues to focus on exposing low-income and minority youngsters to scientific exploration. Located in a church in northeast Portland, ASK-OMSI's popular after school and summer programs are designed to introduce kids to astronomy, chemistry, physics, and other science subjects in a fun, non-threatening atmosphere. The experimental, multi-disciplinary approach to learning science integrates writing, the arts, computers, careers, and cultural awareness into each science subject area.

All of these elements—exhibits, science programs, the Sky Theater and the OMNIMAX—are just the beginning. What visitors see when they walk in the door of the new OMSI will continue to grow and change, and the museum will forever rely on the constant generosity and enthusiasm of the people of the Northwest to support and sustain it.

▪ MARTHA'S BAKED BROWN BREAD ▪

This recipe can be multiplied for a crowd. Following are recipes for 2 loaves and for 10 loaves.

For 2 Loaves:

1½ cups flour
¾ cup sugar
2 teaspoons baking soda
1 teaspoon salt
2 cups whole wheat flour
2 eggs, well beaten
1 cup molasses
1½ cups milk
1 tablespoon vinegar

For 10 Loaves:

7½ cups flour
3¾ cups sugar
3 tablespoons baking soda
1½ tablespoons salt
10 cups whole wheat flour
10 eggs, well beaten
5 cups molasses
7½ cups milk
¼ cup vinegar

Preheat oven to 350 degrees. Grease two **OR** ten 9-inch by 5-inch loaf pans.

Sift together flour, sugar, baking soda and salt into a large bowl. Add whole wheat flour. In a separate bowl stir together eggs, molasses, milk and vinegar until smooth. Add to flour mixture and beat until smooth. Pour batter into prepared pans and bake for 45 minutes, or until toothpick inserted in the center comes out clean. Remove from oven and cool in pans for 5 minutes, then unmold onto a rack to cool completely before slicing.

Connie Hofferber Jones

▪ BROWN BREAD ▪

1½ cups flour
1½ cups rye flour
1 cup cornmeal
1 teaspoon baking soda
1 teaspoon salt
¾ cup chopped walnuts
½ cup raisins
2 cups buttermilk
½ cup dark molasses
Butter

Preheat oven to 375 degrees. Grease two 9-inch by 5-inch loaf pans.

In a large bowl combine flour, rye flour, cornmeal, baking soda and salt and stir to mix well. Stir in walnuts and raisins. Add buttermilk and molasses to dry ingredients, beating well after each addition. Pour batter into prepared pans. Bake for 50 minutes, or until toothpick inserted in the center comes out clean. Remove from oven when done and allow to stand in pans for 5 minutes. Loosen the sides with a knife and turn out onto a rack. Brush top with butter while hot. Cool before slicing.

Toni J. Ives

Recipe for Mice

Dirty shirt
(sweat being the active principle)
Few grains of wheat
Open pot

Place dirty shirt and wheat in open pot. In 21 days mice will appear. The mice will be adults both male and female and will be able to produce mice by mating.

From the Lab of
Jan Babtista Van Helmont
Belgian Philosopher,
Chemist and Physician (1577-1640)

▪ WHEAT GERM ZUCCHINI BREAD ▪

- 3 eggs, beaten
- 1 cup vegetable oil
- 1 cup sugar
- 1 cup brown sugar
- 3 teaspoons maple flavoring **OR** 2 teaspoons vanilla
- 2 cups shredded zucchini
- 2½ cups flour **OR** whole wheat flour
- ½ cup toasted wheat germ
- 2 teaspoons baking soda
- 2 teaspoons salt
- ½ teaspoon baking powder
- 1 cup walnuts, finely chopped

Preheat oven to 350 degrees. Grease and flour two 9-inch by 5-inch loaf pans.

In a large bowl beat eggs until smooth. Add oil, sugar, brown sugar and maple flavoring and continue beating until mixture is thick and foamy. Stir in the zucchini with a spoon. In a separate bowl, stir together flour, wheat germ, baking soda, salt, baking powder and walnuts until well mixed. Gently stir flour mixture into zucchini mixture until just blended. Divide batter between prepared loaf pans. Bake for 1 hour, or until toothpick inserted in the center comes out clean.

Dotti Wilson

"The stillness of the night belies the changes that are occurring on a cosmic scale, for hidden by the vast reaches of space and time is a furious play of power, of forces capable of creating stars and planets—and of destroying them."

—Oregon Symphony Director James DePriest, from the Kendall Planetarium show Cosmic Fury

Mark Bourne

▪ CHEERY CHERRY NUT BREAD ▪

- 2½ cups flour
- 1¼ cups milk
- 1 cup sugar
- 1 cup Cherriannes (dried cherries)
- ½ cup maraschino cherries, sliced or whole
- 1 cup chopped nuts
- 1 egg
- 3 tablespoons vegetable oil
- 3½ teaspoons baking powder
- 1 teaspoon salt

Preheat oven to 350 degrees. Grease and flour a 9-inch by 5-inch bread pan.

Place all ingredients in a large bowl and beat on medium speed for 1 minute, scraping sides constantly, until well blended. Pour into prepared pan and bake for 55 to 65 minutes, or until toothpick inserted in the center comes out clean. Remove from pan and cool completely before slicing.

Wayne and Myrna Simmons
Orchard Crest Farms

▪ BANANA BREAD ▪

½ cup shortening
½ cup sugar
3 eggs
1 teaspoon vanilla extract
2¾ cups flour
1 teaspoon baking powder
¼ teaspoon baking soda
¼ teaspoon salt
1½ cups very ripe bananas, mashed
1 cup chopped nuts

Preheat oven to 350 degrees. Grease and flour two 9-inch by 5-inch by 3-inch loaf pans.

In a large bowl, cream together shortening and sugar until fluffy. Add eggs and vanilla and beat well. Sift together flour, baking powder, baking soda and salt. Add sifted ingredients alternately with mashed bananas to creamed mixture until smooth. Stir in nuts.

Pour batter into prepared pans and bake for about 60 minutes, or until toothpick inserted in the center comes out clean. Cover and cool overnight before slicing.

Blanch E. Zitzewitz

▪ BUTTERMILK SPICE COFFEE CAKE ▪

2½ cups flour
1 cup brown sugar
⅔ cup sugar
⅔ cup vegetable oil
1 cup buttermilk
1 egg, lightly beaten
1½ teaspoons cinnamon
1½ teaspoons nutmeg
1 teaspoon baking soda
½ teaspoon salt

Preheat oven to 350 degrees. Lightly grease and flour a 9-inch by 13-inch cake pan.

In a large bowl, combine flour, brown sugar, sugar and oil. Stir until well blended. Reserve ⅔ cup of this mixture for the topping. Add remaining ingredients to the bowl and mix well. Pour batter into prepared pan and sprinkle reserved topping mixture on top. Bake for 45 to 50 minutes, or until toothpick inserted in the center comes out clean.

Jenny Long

▪ BARA BRITH ▪

This is a traditional Welsh bread.

1 tablespoon active dry yeast
¼ cup warm water (100 degrees to 115 degrees)
2 cups milk, scalded
1 cup currants
1 cup sugar
¼ cup butter
1 teaspoon allspice
1 teaspoon cinnamon
1 teaspoon cloves
1 teaspoon salt
2 eggs, lightly beaten
6 to 6½ cups flour

Preheat oven to 350 degrees. Lightly grease three 8-inch by 4-inch by 2-inch loaf pans.

Dissolve yeast in warm water and allow to proof. Pour the scalded milk into a large bowl and add currants, sugar, butter, allspice, cinnamon, cloves and salt and stir until sugar dissolves. Allow mixture to cool and stir in the yeast mixture and eggs. Stir in enough flour to make a stiff dough. Turn out on a floured board and knead for about 10 minutes, until smooth and satiny. Place dough in a lightly buttered bowl and turn to coat the surface with butter. Cover and set in a warm place to rise until doubled in bulk, about 2 hours.

Punch down dough and divide into 3 large loaves. Put into prepared pans, cover and let rise in a warm place until doubled in bulk.

Bake for 30 to 40 minutes or until the loaves sound hollow when tapped on the top.

Ken Brace
Bryn Seion Welsh Church

▪ HERB BREAD ▪

This recipe is from my fifth grade bread making class, which I took from my math teacher, Mr. Cummings. It became such a favorite at our house, that my parents would ask me to make it for their dinner parties. (And to this day I can still remember how delicious it made the whole house smell!)

½ cup warm water (100 degrees to 115 degrees)
3 packages yeast
2½ cups milk
6 tablespoons sugar
½ cup butter
2 tablespoons salt
8 to 10 cups flour
2 cloves garlic, minced
2 teaspoons dill
2 teaspoons garlic salt
2 teaspoons thyme
1 cup green onions, chopped
1 cup sharp Cheddar cheese, grated

In a large bowl, dissolve yeast in warm water. In a medium sauce pan, combine milk, sugar, butter and salt and heat over low heat until butter melts. Cool to luke-warm and add to yeast mixture. Stir in garlic, dill, garlic salt and thyme. Add flour and stir until dough is too stiff to beat with a spoon. Stir in green onions and cheese. Turn dough out onto a lightly floured surface and knead until smooth and elastic. Place dough in a lightly buttered bowl and turn dough to coat with butter. Cover with a towel and put in a warm place until dough has doubled in bulk, about 1 hour.

Punch down dough and divide into 3 equal portions. Shape dough into round loaves and place on cookie sheets. Cover with a towel and put in a warm place to rise again until dough has doubled in bulk, about 1 hour.

Preheat oven to 375 degrees.

Bake for about 20 minutes. It should have a nice dark crust when fully baked. Let bread sit on a towel for about 10 minutes before slicing. For a lighter crust, brush with butter before baking.

Bridget R. Wise

▪ BREAD MACHINE HERB WHEAT BREAD ▪

1½ teaspoons active dry yeast
1½ cups white bread flour
½ cup wheat bread flour
1 tablespoon powdered skim milk
1 tablespoon margarine **OR** butter
1½ teaspoons garlic powder
1 teaspoon chives, minced
1 teaspoon dill weed
½ teaspoon thyme
½ teaspoon sugar
½ teaspoon salt
1 cup minus 1 tablespoon luke-warm water
¼ cup medium cheddar cheese, grated

Place yeast in the bottom of bread machine pot, toward the edge. Add flours, powdered milk, margarine, garlic powder, chives, dill, thyme, sugar and salt. Add the water on top (water should not touch yeast), and start the machine on medium-brown setting. When machine beeps before the last knead (about 20 minutes), add the cheese. Continue according to manufacturer's directions.

Mary Elizabeth Lyons

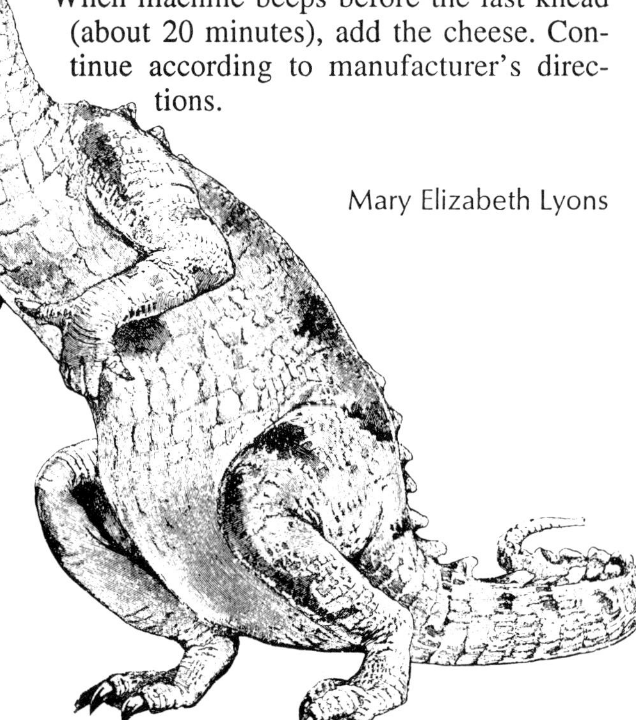

▪ GRANDMA'S BROWN SUGAR ROLLS ▪

My Grandma Bessie Murray was a wonderful cook. Although she seldom measured anything with a standard measuring utensil, every dish she prepared was a treat. This recipe is one of our family favorites; however, I must admit the Brown Sugar Rolls always tasted better at Grandma's house when we ate them for breakfast instead of toast.

1¾ cups flour
2½ teaspoons baking powder
¾ teaspoon salt
⅓ cup shortening
¾ cup milk, approximately
Butter
Brown sugar

Preheat oven to 350 degrees. Lightly grease a baking sheet.

In a large bowl, sift together flour, baking powder and salt. Add the shortening and blend with a pastry cutter or fork until the mixture resembles coarse meal. Stir in just enough milk so that dough pulls away from the sides of the bowl and holds together.

Turn dough out onto a lightly floured board and knead gently ten times. Roll out dough into a rectangle about ¼-inch to ½-inch thick. Spread with butter and sprinkle with brown sugar. Roll up dough and cut into 1-inch slices. Place sliced rolls, cut side down, on prepared baking sheet. Bake for about 30 minutes or until lightly brown. Do not overcook.

Grandma's Brown Sugar Rolls were always served hot with lots of love. I hope that you, too, enjoy serving our family favorite the same way.

The Honorable Barbara Roberts
Governor of Oregon

▪ ORANGE ROLLS ▪

Orange Rolls:

1 cake yeast **OR** 1 package dry yeast
¼ cup warm water (100 degrees to 115 degrees)
1½ cups milk
½ cup sugar
3 tablespoons shortening
1 teaspoon salt
¼ cup orange juice*
2 tablespoons orange zest, minced
2 eggs, beaten
5 cups flour

Orange Icing:

1 cup powdered sugar
2 tablespoons orange juice*
1 teaspoon orange zest, minced

Preheat oven to 375 degrees. Grease a 9-inch by 13-inch baking pan.

Dissolve the yeast in the warm water and allow to proof. Combine milk, sugar, shortening and salt in a sauce pan and scald. Remove from heat and pour into a large bowl. Allow to cool to lukewarm. Stir in dissolved yeast, orange juice, orange zest and eggs until well blended. Stir in the flour until well incorporated and let stand 10 minutes. Turn out dough onto a lightly floured surface and knead until smooth and elastic. Place in a greased bowl and turn so that the surface is coated. Cover with a towel and place in a warm spot for 2 hours, or until doubled in bulk.

Turn out dough onto a lightly floured surface and roll out to about ½-inch thickness. Cut in strips, 8-inches long by ¾-inch wide. Tie into a loose knot and place in prepared baking pan. Cover and let rise again until doubled in bulk. Bake for 15 to 20 minutes, or until golden brown. Remove from oven and, using a pastry brush, ice immediately with Orange Icing.

Prepare Orange Icing by combining powdered sugar, orange juice and orange zest until smooth.

*For extra orange flavor, use frozen orange juice concentrate mixed with only half the amount of water called for.

Charles W. Manke

▪ CINNAMON TOAST COFFEE CAKE ▪

If you wake up your family on Sunday morning with this coffee cake, they will give you BIG hugs!

Coffee Cake:

2 cups flour
1 cup sugar
2 teaspoons baking powder
1 teaspoon salt
½ teaspoon cinnamon
¼ teaspoon nutmeg
1 cup milk
2 tablespoons melted butter
1 teaspoon vanilla
¾ cup raisins

Topping:

½ cup sugar
1½ tablespoons cinnamon
½ cup melted butter
½ cup chopped walnuts

Preheat oven to 350 degrees. Grease and flour a 9-inch by 13-inch pan.

For the Coffee Cake:

In a large bowl, stir together the flour, 1 cup sugar, baking powder, salt, ½ teaspoon cinnamon and nutmeg until well blended. Add milk, 2 tablespoons butter and vanilla and beat until smooth. Stir in raisins.

For the Topping:

In a medium bowl, stir together the ½ cup sugar and the 1½ teaspoons cinnamon until well blended. Stir in ½ cup melted butter and walnuts and stir until well combined.

Pour batter into prepared pan. Bake for 10 minutes then remove from oven and sprinkle Topping over batter. Return to oven and bake an additional 20 to 25 minutes, or until a toothpick inserted in the center comes out clean. Serves 8 to 10.

Toni J. Ives

Hancock Field Station Director Joseph Jones shows the articulating surface of a large mammal femur bone to students at summer camp.

▪ CINNAMON FLATBREAD ▪

1¼ cups flour
¾ cup whole wheat flour
1 tablespoon sugar
2 teaspoons baking powder
½ teaspoon baking soda
⅓ cup sesame seeds
2 tablespoons cold butter
1 cup plain yogurt
½ cup raisins
2 tablespoons butter, melted
2 tablespoons sugar
1½ teaspoons cinnamon

Preheat oven to 425 degrees. Lightly grease a round pizza pan.

In a large bowl, sift together the flour, whole wheat flour, 1 tablespoon sugar, baking powder and baking soda. Stir in the sesame seeds. Add 2 tablespoons cold butter and cut into flour mixture with a pastry blender or fork until the mixture resembles coarse meal. Add yogurt and raisins and mix well. Turn out onto lightly floured board and knead for a few minutes, or until slightly springy.

Pat dough out evenly onto prepared pizza pan. Bake for about 10 minutes, or until lightly browned. Remove from oven and brush with 2 tablespoons melted butter. In a small bowl, combine 2 tablespoons sugar and cinnamon and stir with a fork. Sprinkle mixture evenly over melted butter. Return to oven and bake an additional 5 to 10 minutes. Serve warm in wedges.

Jenny Long

▪ LEFSA ▪

3 cups potatoes; peeled, boiled and mashed
¼ teaspoon salt
2 tablespoons melted butter
¾ cup flour

Heat griddle to 450 degrees.

In a large bowl, mix potatoes, salt and butter until smooth. Stir in flour and form into a ball. Cover with waxed paper and let cool completely.

On a lightly floured board, roll out a piece of dough, the size of a golf ball, into an oval until it is almost thin enough to see through. Carefully lift the Lefsa and place on the hot, ungreased griddle. Let it cook until the bottom is covered with brown spots. Turn over and cook until other side is completely baked and covered with brown spots. Let cool before wrapping in waxed paper to keep them fresh and soft.

To serve, spread warm Lefsa with butter then sprinkle with sugar, brown sugar or jam. Roll up and enjoy.

Francis C. Berg

▪ WELSH CAKES ▪

1½ cups sugar
1 cup margarine **OR** butter
2 eggs
¼ cup orange juice
4 cups flour
3 teaspoons baking powder
½ teaspoon nutmeg
½ teaspoon salt
¼ teaspoon baking soda
¾ cup currants
Additional sugar

Heat a griddle to 350 degrees.

In a large bowl, cream together the sugar, margarine, eggs and orange juice. Sift together flour, baking powder, nutmeg, salt and baking soda and stir into creamed mixture. Stir in the currants. Turn out dough onto lightly floured surface and roll out to about ½-inch thick. Cut into circles with a 2½-inch round cookie cutter or glass.

Place on hot griddle, and cook on both sides until golden brown. Dip hot Welsh Cakes in sugar on both sides.

Ken and Dorothy Brace

Honey

Honey comes out of the air. . . . At early dawn the leaves of trees are found bedewed with honey. . . . Whether this is the perspiration of the sky or a sort of saliva of the stars, or the moisture of the air purging itself, nevertheless it brings with it the great pleasure of it's heavenly nature. It is always of the best quality when it is stored in the best flowers.

Pliny

▪ GERMAN PANCAKES ▪

This is great for brunch or supper. One pancake feeds one adult.

2 tablespoons butter
3 eggs
½ teaspoon salt
½ cup flour
½ cup milk

Preheat oven to 450 degrees. Spread 2 tablespoons butter in the bottom and sides of a 9-inch cake pan.

In a large bowl, beat the eggs until very light. Add the salt and flour, beating constantly. Slowly pour in the milk, beating until smooth. Pour the batter into prepared pan and bake for about 20 minutes. Reduce heat to 350 degrees and continue baking for about 5 minutes, or until crisp and golden brown. The sides will have risen high. Traditionally served with lemon and powdered sugar, but also good with syrup. Makcs one pancake.

Susan Sokol Blosser
Sokol Blosser Winery

▪ RICOTTA PANCAKES ▪

⅔ cup ricotta cheese
2 egg yolks
¼ cup milk
6 tablespoons flour
1 tablespoon sugar
¼ teaspoon baking powder
¼ teaspoon salt
2 egg whites, beaten until stiff

Preheat griddle to 350 degrees. Grease lightly.

In a large bowl, blend ricotta, egg yolks and milk until smooth. Sift together flour, sugar, baking powder and salt and stir into ricotta mixture until just incorporated. Fold egg whites into batter, taking care not to deflate egg whites as much as possible.

Pour about ¼ cup batter per pancake onto prepared griddle. Cook until a few bubbles break on top and bottom is golden. Turn the pancakes over and cook until the bottoms are golden brown. Serve hot with blueberry or maple syrup. Makes 8 pancakes

Anne Amdahl

Why does aluminum foil hurt when you chew it?

The pain we feel is actually a tiny electrical shock, when your mouth sets up the properties of a battery. A small electric current is created when the two metals from the fillings in your teeth and thc aluminum foil come in contact with saliva. The metals react to produce positive and negative charges and the electrical current flows throw the saliva, shocking your tongue and cheeks along the way.

David Heil
Newton's Apple
Associate Director, OMSI

▪ CUSTARD PANCAKES ▪

This has been a favorite in my husband's family since he was a little boy. We recently introduced this recipe to close friends who own a bed and breakfast in Portland, Oregon, called the John Palmer House. Mary Sauter (the owner) says that it is one of the guests' favorites. Mary prepares this dish in individual casseroles so that each portion can be baked as the guests come down for breakfast. This makes for a pretty presentation with some fresh fruit as a garnish.

3 eggs
2 cups milk
1 cup flour
1 tablespoon sugar
1/8 teaspoon salt
Powdered Sugar
Syrup or jam as an accompaniment

Preheat oven to 475 degrees. Lightly butter a 9-inch by 13-inch pan.

Combine all ingredients in a large bowl and mix well. Pour batter into prepared pan. Bake for 20 minutes. Remove from oven and sprinkle with powdered sugar. Cut into squares and serve with syrup or jam.

Kathleen and Tom McKnight

▪ BUTTER AND ORANGE FLUFFY ▪

Use on pancakes, waffles, toast or biscuits.

1/2 cup butter, at room temperature
1/2 cup brown sugar
2 teaspoons orange zest, minced

In a large bowl, cream butter until light and fluffy. Add brown sugar gradually, beating the mixture into a light and fluffy mass. Stir in the orange zest.

Toni J. Ives

CAKES

▪ Pacific Rim Spaceflight Academy ▪

Project Gemini and Shuttle Mission are exciting five-day camps at OMSI's Education Resource Center that recreate the excitement of America's space program for 9 to 18 year olds. Using OMSI's replica Gemini spacecraft and it's shuttle flight deck in the Space Science Hall, participants train for simulated space missions. Training includes the study of the science and technology involved in spaceflight, model rocketry, and SCUBA and snorkeling to experience working in a weightless environment while assembling a simulated space station under water. Gemini campers take off in and airplane while the pilot performs zero-gravity maneuver, and Shuttle Mission campers soar in a glider which, like the Space Shuttle, returns to Earth for an unpowered landing.

Connie Hofferber Jones

▪ APPLE CAKE ▪

This cake can be multiplied for a crowd. Following are recipes for 1 cake and for 8 cakes.

For 1 Cake:

4 cups diced apples
2 cups sugar
Juice of ½ lemon
½ cup vegetable oil
2 eggs, beaten
2 teaspoons vanilla
1 cup chopped nuts
2 cups flour
2 teaspoons baking soda
2 teaspoons cinnamon
½ teaspoon salt

For 8 Cakes:

2 gallons diced apples
16 cups sugar
Juice of 4 lemons
4 cups vegetable oil
16 eggs, beaten
5 tablespoons vanilla
8 cups chopped nuts
16 cups flour
5 tablespoons baking soda
5 tablespoons cinnamon
4 teaspoons salt

Preheat oven to 350 degrees. Grease and flour one OR eight 9-inch by 13-inch baking pans.

In a large bowl, toss together apples, sugar and lemon juice. Add oil, eggs, vanilla and nuts and stir to combine. Sift together flour, baking soda, cinnamon and salt and add to apple mixture. Blend until smooth. Pour into prepared pan and bake for 1 hour, or until toothpick inserted in the center comes out clean. When cool, dust with powdered sugar.

Connie Hofferber Jones

Sticky Food

In the weightless environment of space, floating crumbs can be an annoyance if not a hazard. Floating liquids are even more dangerous because they can short out electrical equipment. The menu aboard the space shuttle is planned to avoid floating food. Food that crumbles or that is likely to lead to small floating debris is left on Earth. In the early days of space travel, pureed food was squeezed from tubes to avoid loose food in the spacecraft cabin. Today aboard the space shuttle, astronauts eat many ordinary foods but entrees usually contain a sauce or sticky substance that adheres food to eating utensils.

Rob Grover

▪ BABOUSAH ▪

(BAS-BOO-SAH)

1 cup plain yogurt
½ cup fruit juice concentrate **OR** honey
2½ cups farina, uncooked (Cream of Wheat)
2 teaspoons vanilla
1 teaspoon baking soda
½ cup melted butter
1 cup raisins

Preheat oven to 350 degrees. Butter a 9-inch by 9-inch baking pan.

In a large bowl, blend the yogurt and fruit juice concentrate together. Stir in the farina until smooth. Add the vanilla, baking soda and butter and mix until smooth. Stir in raisins. Spread batter into prepared baking pan and bake for 30 minutes, or until golden brown. Remove from oven and cover with foil until cool.

Surra Tregarth

▪ PRUNE CAKE ▪

This recipe is from my grandmother Richardson and is one of our favorites.

Prune Cake:

1½ cups pitted prunes
1 cup sugar
⅔ cup shortening
1½ cups flour
1 teaspoon allspice
1 teaspoon cinnamon
1 teaspoon nutmeg
½ teaspoon salt
3 egg yolks
1 egg white
¼ cup sour cream
1 teaspoon baking soda
1 teaspoon vanilla

Frosting:

2 cups powdered sugar
⅓ cup water
¼ teaspoon cream of tartar
2 egg whites, stiffly beaten
½ teaspoon vanilla

Preheat oven to 375 degrees. Grease and flour an 8-inch by 8-inch baking pan.

For the Prune Cake:

Place prunes in a small sauce pan and barely cover with water. Simmer over low heat until very tender. Drain prunes and save the liquid. Mash or puree prunes thoroughly.

In a large bowl, cream together the sugar and shortening. Stir in the mashed prunes. Sift the flour, allspice, cinnamon, nutmeg and salt into the creamed mixture. Blend until smooth. Beat in the egg yolks and egg white. Dissolve the baking soda in the sour cream and add to mixture. Add vanilla and blend until smooth. If batter is too stiff, add enough reserved prune liquid to make the batter smooth and pourable. Pour batter into prepared pan and bake for 40 minutes, or until toothpick inserted in the center comes out clean. Cool completely and frost.

For the Frosting:

Place powdered sugar, water and cream of tartar in a sauce pan. Bring to a boil and boil for 2 minutes. Pour syrup into stiffly beaten egg whites in a thin stream, beating constantly. Add vanilla and beat until smooth and fluffy.

Lois Keefe

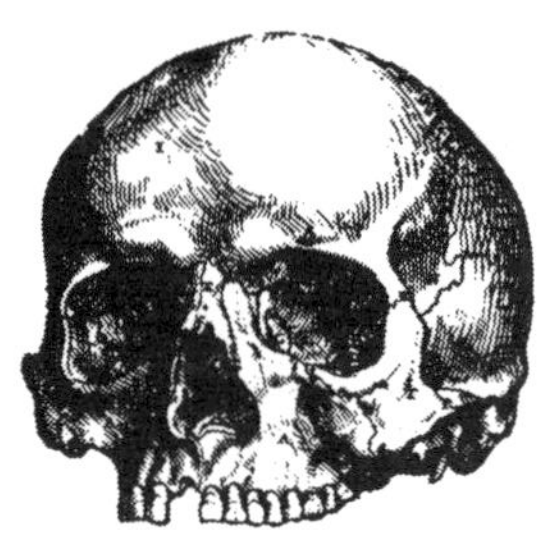

▪ CHOCOLATE SAUERKRAUT CAKE ▪

⅔ cup margarine **OR** butter
1½ cups sugar
3 eggs
1 teaspoon vanilla
½ cup unsweetened cocoa powder
2¼ cups flour
1 teaspoon baking powder
1 teaspoon baking soda
¼ teaspoon salt
1 cup water
1 cup Steinfeld's Sauerkraut, rinsed and drained

Preheat oven to 350 degrees. Grease and flour two 9-inch round cake pans or one 9-inch by 13-inch pan.

In a large bowl, thoroughly cream together margarine and sugar. Beat in eggs and vanilla. Sift together dry ingredients and add alternately with water to creamed mixture. Stir in sauerkraut. Pour batter into prepared pans and bake for 25 to 30 minutes, or until a toothpick inserted in the center comes out clean. Cool completely and frost with favorite frosting.

Ray Steinfeld, Jr.
Steinfeld's Products Company

▪ GRANDMA STELLA'S MOLASSES CAKE ▪

My maternal grandmother was very important to me when I was growing up in Michigan, particularly in my early teens. Stella was simple, sweet, and down to earth—like her molasses cake! Stella's great-granddaughter, Lisa, makes a perfect lemon sauce to top it that the great-great grandchildren love. (It's also delicious with homemade whipped cream or ice cream.)

1½ cups flour
½ cup sugar
½ cup lard **OR** margarine
1 egg
1 teaspoon cinnamon
1 scant teaspoon salt
½ teaspoon ginger
½ cup molasses
1 teaspoon baking soda
¾ cup boiling water

Preheat oven to 350 degrees. Grease and flour an 8-inch square baking pan.

In a large bowl, mix flour, sugar, lard, egg, cinnamon, salt and ginger until smooth. In a measuring cup, measure molasses, then add baking soda and stir until molasses turns a light tan color (usually a couple of minutes). Add to flour mixture and blend. Add boiling water and beat until smooth.

Pour into prepared pan and bake for 25 to 40 minutes, or until toothpick inserted in the center comes out clean. (Time varies according to altitude; higher altitude requires longer baking time.) This is especially good if you put it in the oven before dinner, then eat it warm when dinner is over.

Tangy Lemon Sauce

⅔ cup sugar
1 tablespoon—or more—cornstarch
1 cup boiling water
2 tablespoons lemon juice
1 teaspoon lemon rind
2 tablespoons butter
Few grains of salt

Combine cornstarch and sugar in pan over medium heat. Add boiling water and stir vigorously until it thickens. Stir often. When it thickens, remove from heat, stir in juice, rind, butter and salt. Pour warm over molasses cake.

William W. Lyons

▪ APPLE AND BANANA CAKE ▪

4 cups apples; peeled, cored and diced
2 cups sugar
2 ripe bananas, diced
1 cup nuts, chopped
½ cup vegetable oil
2 eggs, lightly beaten
2 teaspoons vanilla
2 cups flour
2 teaspoons cinnamon
2 teaspoons baking soda
1 teaspoon salt

Preheat oven to 350 degrees. Grease and flour a 9-inch by 13-inch cake pan.

In a large bowl, combine apples, sugar and bananas and toss to coat well. Set aside. In a separate bowl, combine nuts, oil, eggs and vanilla and mix well. Stir into apple mixture and blend well. Sift together flour, cinnamon, baking soda and salt into the batter and mix well. Pour batter into prepared pan and bake for about 1 hour, or until toothpick inserted in the center comes out clean. Cool completely before frosting.

Frosting:

5 tablespoons flour
¼ teaspoon salt
1 cup milk
1 cup butter **OR** margarine, softened
1 cup sugar
1 teaspoon vanilla

Place flour and salt in the top of a double-boiler. Add milk in a thin stream, whisking constantly. Cook over boiling water, whisking constantly, until mixture thickens. Remove from heat and cool completely.

In a large bowl, combine cooled mixture, butter, sugar and vanilla. Beat until mixture is light and fluffy.

Lynda Johnston

▪ OLDE MRS. WHIPPLE'S APPLE GINGERBREAD ▪

This recipe comes from my great, great, great, great, great, great grandmother, Frances Edwards Whipple.

1 cup molasses
½ cup shortening
½ cup sugar
1 egg
2½ cups flour
1½ teaspoons ginger
1 teaspoon cinnamon
1 teaspoon coriander
1 teaspoon nutmeg
½ teaspoon salt
1 cup boiling water
1 tablespoon baking soda
1 medium apple; peeled, cored and finely chopped
Whipped cream or ice cream as an accompaniment

Preheat oven to 350 degrees. Grease and flour a 9-inch by 13-inch cake pan.

In a large bowl, cream together the molasses, shortening, sugar and egg until smooth. In a separate bowl, sift together the flour, ginger, cinnamon, coriander, nutmeg and salt. Add to creamed mixture and mix well. Dissolve baking soda in the boiling water and add to mixture and blend well. Stir in apples.

Pour batter into prepared pan and bake for about 1 hour. This makes a very moist cake and is wonderful served with whipped cream or ice cream.

Blaine Whipple

Early OMSI Happenings

Because OMSI started on such a small scale a few staff and volunteers had to be creative and versatile to accomplish special events and fund raisers.

After the first auction, ZOOMSI (Zoo and OMSI), we were not prepared to do a night deposit. We had collected the receipts in a cigar box and one loyal board member guarded it overnight under his bed until we could get it to the bank the following day. Auctions were always a team effort.

One OMSI Auction was held at a local ice rink. Even though the ice had been removed, we all had cold feet. The first "Written Bid" idea started that year and it was so popular we were just swamped in cashiering and had to record the high bidders at home and bring the receipts back for the second night's auction.

Camp Hancock was another joint effort. We all pitched in to help with shopping and set-up as well as building projects. Our insurance company organized a building project team almost every summer to build and maintain the camp.

Many Science Fairs were held at OMSI. Staff and volunteers burned the midnight oil after judging was done to prepare lists, awards and report to the newspaper.

Epicurean Experience was a wild experience the first two years. It was held at OMSI and had to be set up after the school tours were out of the building. We had to convert the main floor into a restaurant in a matter of a few hours. Borrowed tables, chairs, dishes and linens had to be put in place. Decorating, signs, floral arrangements, foods and wines had to be in place by 6:00 pm that evening. In addition, it was necessary to set up dish and glass rinsing stations downstairs. Since there were 15 to 20 food stations, each with appropriate plates, there were lots of dishes to do. Then after the party, the building had to be set up for business the next day.

In spite of all the work and deadlines to be met, OMSI was always a fun place to work and it attracted a wonderful group of willing staff and volunteers.

Barbara Curtis

▪ GERRY'S CHOCOLATE CAKE ▪

Cake:

2½ cups flour
1½ teaspoons baking soda
1 teaspoon baking powder
½ cup cocoa powder
½ teaspoon salt
⅔ cup butter
1⅓ cups sugar
2 eggs
½ cup water
3 teaspoons vanilla
1 cup buttermilk

Frosting:

1 6-ounce package chocolate chips
½ cup half-and-half
1 cup butter
2½ cups powdered sugar

Preheat oven to 350 degrees. Butter and flour two 9-inch round cake pans. Line the bottom with waxed or parchment paper and butter and flour the paper.

For the Cake:

Sift together the flour, baking soda, baking powder, cocoa and salt. Set aside.

In the bowl of an electric mixer, cream the butter. Gradually add the eggs, one at a time, beating 1 minute after each egg. Gradually add water and vanilla and beat for 1 minute. Do not overbeat.

With the mixer on low speed, alternately add the sifted flour mixture and buttermilk. (Add the flour mixture in four parts, buttermilk in three, beginning and ending with the flour.) Blend only until the flour no longer shows. Do not overbeat.

Pour the batter into the prepared pans and tap once to settle the batter. Bake for 30 minutes, or until a toothpick inserted in the center comes out clean. Cool the cakes for 10 minutes before inverting on wire racks. Cool completely before frosting.

For the Frosting:

Combine the chocolate chips, half-and-half and butter in a saucepan over medium heat, stirring constantly until the mixture is smooth. Whisk in the powdered sugar. In a bowl, set over ice, beat the icing with a wire whisk until the frosting holds it's shape, about 10 minutes.

Makes 1 cake. (10 to 12 servings).

Gerald W. Frank

Taste Buds in Space

If you are a chocolate lover, space may not be the place for you. Susan Helms, a Portland native and shuttle astronaut reported during a visit to OMSI that chocolate in space had a disappointingly metallic taste. American Skylab astronauts found themselves craving spicy foods and a Russian cosmonaut, after being in space for nearly a year, craved lemons.

Rob Grover

▪ BOLEY CAKE ▪

2 cups unsweetened applesauce
1½ teaspoons baking soda
1 cup shortening **OR** margarine
1½ cups sugar
⅓ cup cocoa powder
1 teaspoon cinnamon
½ teaspoon salt
½ teaspoon vanilla
¼ teaspoon cloves
2 cups flour
½ cup raisins **OR** chopped dates **OR** chopped nuts

Preheat oven to 350 degrees. Grease and flour a 9-inch by 13-inch cake pan.

Heat applesauce in a small pan over medium heat. When hot, remove from heat and stir in baking soda. Pour applesauce mixture into a large bowl. Add shortening, sugar, cocoa, cinnamon, salt, vanilla and cloves and mix well. Add flour and mix until smooth. Stir in raisins. Pour batter into prepared pan and bake for 45 minutes, or until toothpick inserted in the center comes out clean.

Optional:

When cool, frost with cream cheese icing.

Melinda Dow

▪ RHUBARB CHEESECAKE ▪

This recipe was awarded the 1993 "People's Choice" during OMSI's 19th Annual Epicurean Experience.

Crust:

1 cup flour
½ cup walnuts, finely chopped
2 tablespoons sugar
⅓ cup butter

Preheat oven to 350 degrees. Butter and flour a 9-inch springform pan.

Mix together flour, walnuts and sugar in a large bowl. Add butter and cut in with a fork or pastry cutter until mixture resembles oatmeal. Press dough into the bottom of prepared springform pan. Bake for 10 to 12 minutes, or until set and lightly browned. Remove and cool.

Filling:

2 pounds cream cheese, at room temperature
¾ cup sugar
2 teaspoons vanilla
4 eggs

In the bowl of an electric mixer, cream together the cream cheese and sugar on medium speed. Add the vanilla. Add the eggs, one at a time, blending well and scraping down the sides of the bowl after each addition. Mix until smooth. Pour into the baked crust and put on the topping.

Topping:

1 cup walnuts, coarsely chopped
¾ cup sugar
1 teaspoon cinnamon
3 to 4 stalks rhubarb, sliced thinly at a sharp angle
¼ cup sugar

In a small bowl, combine the walnuts, ¾ cup sugar and cinnamon and mix well. In a separate bowl, toss the rhubarb with the ¼ cup sugar. Spread half of the walnut mixture on top of the cheesecake. Arrange the rhubarb slices symmetrically on top, and sprinkle remaining walnut mixture on top. Bake at 350 degrees for about 45 minutes. Cool at room temperature and refrigerate for at least 3 hours or overnight. Serve with Rhubarb Sauce.

Rhubarb Sauce:

1 pound rhubarb stalks, cut into 1-inch pieces
½ cup sugar
¼ cup water
1 teaspoon lemon zest

Combine all ingredients in a large sauce pan. Simmer over low heat until rhubarb is very tender. Can be served warm or cold.

Kathryn L. Bliss CWC, CCE
Maxi's Restaurant
Portland, Oregon

Baking Soda and Baking Powder

Baking soda (sodium bicarbonate) is an alkaline chemical leavening agent that reacts with acidic ingredients, such as buttermilk or molasses, to create carbon dioxide. The resulting gas bubbles in the batters give products, such as cakes, a light texture.

Double-acting baking powder contains baking soda and acid salts, sodium aluminum sulfate and calcium acid phosphate, that begin to react as soon as they come in contact with liquid to form carbon dioxide. They produce a second, and greater set of gas bubbles during baking.

To test the effectiveness of baking powder, mix 1 teaspoon baking powder with ⅓ cup hot water; it should bubble vigorously.

If you run out of baking powder you can mix together ½ teaspoon cream of tartar and ⅓ teaspoon baking soda and ⅛ teaspoon salt to equal 1 teaspoon baking powder.

▪ BUTTERMILK CAKE ▪

Cake:

1½ cups sugar
½ cup butter or margarine
¼ cup vegetable oil
2 eggs
1 cup Oregon Prunes, chopped
1 teaspoon vanilla
2 cups flour
1 teaspoon baking soda
1 teaspoon allspice
1 teaspoon cinnamon
1 teaspoon nutmeg
1 teaspoon salt
1 cup buttermilk

Preheat oven to 350 degrees. Grease and flour a 9-inch by 13-inch pan.

In a large bowl, beat together sugar, butter, oil and eggs until smooth. Blend in the prunes and vanilla. Add the flour, baking soda, allspice, cinnamon, nutmeg and salt and mix thoroughly. Stir in buttermilk and beat until smooth. Pour into prepared pan and bake for 35 to 40 minutes, or until toothpick inserted in the center comes out clean. Pour topping over the cake as soon as you take it out of the oven. Let stand for at least 1 hour before serving to allow the topping to soak into the cake.

Topping:

1 cup sugar
½ cup butter or margarine
½ cup buttermilk
½ teaspoon baking soda
½ teaspoon vanilla

Place all ingredients in a medium sauce pan and stir to blend well. Bring to a boil over medium heat and cook for 2 minutes. Pour topping over cake.

Wayne and Myrna Simmons
Orchard Crest Farms

▪ SACHTER FAMILY CHEESECAKE ▪

20 zwieback crackers
2 tablespoons sugar
2 tablespoons unsalted butter
4 egg yolks,
2 tablespoons flour
2 tablespoons sugar
1 teaspoon vanilla
⅛ teaspoon salt
12 ounces cream cheese
1 cup sugar
1 cup sour cream
4 egg whites, stiffly beaten

Preheat oven to 350 degrees. Butter a 12-inch springform pan very well.

Crush the zwieback crackers to very fine crumbs. Combine crumbs with 2 tablespoons sugar and butter and press into the prepared springform pan. Set aside.

In a medium bowl, beat the egg yolks until thick and lemon-colored, about 8 minutes. Beat in flour, 2 tablespoons sugar, vanilla and salt.

In a large bowl, cream together the cream cheese and 1 cup sugar until smooth. Add egg yolk mixture to cream cheese mixture and blend well. Add sour cream and blend until smooth. Carefully fold in beaten egg whites, taking care to deflate as little as possible.

Pour mixture into prepared springform pan. Bake for 1 hour. When finished, turn off oven but do not open oven for an additional hour. Remove and allow to cool. Unmold and chill thoroughly before serving.

Ruth Sachter

▪ PUMPKIN SPICE CAKE ▪

1⅓ cups sugar
½ cup shortening
2 eggs
1 cup pumpkin, cooked and pureed
⅔ cup buttermilk
1¾ cups flour
2 teaspoons baking powder
2 teaspoons cinnamon
1 teaspoon baking soda
1 teaspoon salt
½ teaspoon nutmeg
¼ teaspoon allspice
¼ teaspoon ginger

Frosting:

2 cups powdered sugar
⅓ cup butter, softened
1 egg yolk, very fresh
1 teaspoon vanilla extract
1 cup powdered sugar
A few drops cream

Preheat oven to 350 degrees. Grease and flour a 9-inch by 13-inch baking pan.

For the Cake:

In a large bowl, cream together the sugar and shortening. Add eggs one at a time, beating well after each addition. In a separate bowl, stir together the pumpkin and buttermilk until smooth. In a separate bowl, sift together the flour, baking powder, cinnamon, baking soda, salt, nutmeg, allspice and ginger. Add pumpkin mixture to creamed mixture alternately with the sifted ingredients, blending well after each addition.

Pour batter into prepared pan and bake for about 40 to 45 minutes, or until toothpick inserted in the center comes out clean. Cool completely before frosting.

For the Frosting:

In a medium bowl, cream 2 cups of the powdered sugar with the butter until light and fluffy. Add the egg yolk and vanilla and beat until blended. Add the remaining 1 cup powdered sugar and blend until smooth. Beat in a few drops of cream until frosting is a spreading consistency. Spread on cooled cake. Store in the refrigerator.

Carolyn Rose

▪ GRAHAM CRACKER CAKE ▪

This recipe is a family favorite. I won a champion ribbon for this cake in 1972 when I was 10 years old at a 4-H competition.

1¾ cups graham cracker crumbs
1 cup sugar
⅓ cup flour
2 teaspoons baking powder
1 cup milk
¾ cup almonds **OR** walnuts, chopped
½ cup butter **OR** margarine, softened
2 eggs
1 teaspoon vanilla

Topping:

½ cup sugar
½ teaspoon cinnamon
¼ cup butter
½ cup heavy cream **OR** evaporated milk

Preheat oven to 375 degrees. Grease and flour a 9-inch square pan.

For the Cake:

In a large bowl, stir together the graham cracker crumbs, sugar, flour and baking powder until well combined. Add the milk, nuts, butter, eggs and vanilla and beat on medium speed with a mixer until thoroughly blended. Pour batter into prepared pan and bake for about 45 minutes, or until edges just start pulling away from the pan and toothpick inserted in the center comes out clean. While the cake is baking, prepare topping.

For the Topping:

In a medium saucepan, stir together sugar and cinnamon. Add butter and cream. Bring to a boil over high heat, whisking constantly. Boil for 1 minute, whisking constantly.

Remove cake from the oven. Prick cake gently all over with a fork and pour topping over cake, allowing it to soak in. Serve warm or cooled.

Kim Kaseberg Decker

▪ OATMEAL CAKE ▪

Cake:

1 cup oatmeal
1½ cups boiling water
1½ cups flour
1 cup sugar
1 cup brown sugar
½ cup vegetable oil
2 eggs
1 teaspoon baking soda
½ teaspoon cinnamon

Topping:

1 cup shredded coconut
1 cup walnuts, chopped
½ cup heavy cream **OR** evaporated milk
½ cup brown sugar
6 tablespoons butter
1 teaspoon vanilla

Preheat oven to 350 degrees. Grease a 9-inch by 13-inch baking pan.

For the Cake:

Combine oatmeal and boiling water in a large bowl. Let stand for 5 minutes. In a separate bowl, combine flour, sugar, brown sugar, oil, eggs, baking soda and cinnamon and mix well. Add to oatmeal mixture and blend well. Pour into prepared pan and bake for 25 to 30 minutes, or until toothpick inserted in the center comes out clean.

For the Topping:

Combine topping ingredients in a medium saucepan. Stir over low heat until butter melts and brown sugar dissolves. Spread topping over hot cake and put under the broiler until golden brown and bubbly. Cool and cut into small squares.

Bernadette McChrystal

▪ NORWEGIAN CARAMEL AND ALMOND TOSCA CAKE ▪

My husband, Frank, is of Norwegian-American descent, and a long-time member of the Sons of Norway. I was instructed in the preparation of this recipe by his grandmother in her kitchen in Lincoln, Nebraska.

Cake:

3 eggs
1 cup sugar
1 teaspoon vanilla
1½ cups flour
1½ teaspoons baking powder
¼ cup butter, melted
3 tablespoons milk

Topping:

¼ cup butter
½ cup slivered blanched almonds
½ cup sugar
½ cup heavy cream

Preheat oven to 350 degrees. Butter an 11-inch springform pan.

For the Cake:

Place eggs in a large bowl, and beat until foamy. Add sugar and beat until light and pale-colored. Stir in vanilla. Sift flour and baking powder into mixture and blend well. Mix ¼ cup melted butter and milk together then add to mixture and blend until smooth. Pour batter into prepared springform pan and bake for 30 to 35 minutes, or until toothpick inserted in the center comes out clean. Cool.

For the Topping:

Place ¼ cup butter in a heavy sauce pan and melt over medium heat. Add almonds and sauté until almonds are golden. Add ½ cup sugar and cream and stir to blend. Increase heat to high and bring mixture to a boil, whisking constantly. Boil, whisking constantly, for about 3 minutes, or until mixture thickens slightly and begins to turn golden. Pour hot topping mixture over cake and place under the broiler until topping begins to bubble and turn a caramel color. Serves 10.

Karen A. Krone

PASTRIES

▪ Hancock Field Station ▪

Hancock Field Station is OMSI's oldest camp and is owned by the museum. Located within the boundaries of the John Day Fossil Beds National Monument, the field station was founded in 1951 by A. W. (Lon) Hancock, an amateur paleontologist and geologist from Portland, who unearthed fossils of rhinoceros, camels, alligators, big cats, tiny horses and giant *brontotherium* in the area. He had been bringing youngsters from his neighborhood to these hills for years to help him with this digging and in 1951 formalized the outings with OMSI sponsorship and leadership by university geologists.

Hancock Field Station is nestled among rolling hills of juniper-sage grassland, just two miles from the John Day River. The six dormitory-style cabins are wooden A-frames, each holding 12 wooden bunks with mattresses. Separate bathroom and shower facilities for women and men are centrally located. The screened dining hall seats 75 comfortably and is attached to a modern kitchen. The educational facilities include several laboratories, a well-stocked natural sciences library, a darkroom, and a lapidary workshop. A medical dispensary is equipped for emergencies and minor health problems.

Hancock's educational year runs from March to November with students from first grade through graduate school coming from throughout Washington and Oregon during the spring and fall. They study geology, arid grassland, forest, and stream ecology for three to five days. Research is an added dimension here: All students, no matter what age, dig fossils and record them in an on-going paleontology research project of the Bridge Creek flora, or they study the health of nearby Pine Creek by measuring dissolved oxygen, pH, stream flow, and diversity of life in the water.

By June summer camps have started: week long canoe trips down the John Day River, backpack trips into the Wallowa Mountains, investigations of the ancient forests of Oregon, canoeing on the Cascade lakes, wilderness survival experiences on Mount Hood, training in the ways the Native Americans lived in these areas long ago, and understanding how plants and animals have adapted to living in this dry environment. Some of the 15 summer camp programs are Hancock-based, others are totally in the wilderness, and some range to Wyoming, Alaska, and the Southwest.

In addition, Hancock Field Station serves as a base camp for many university researchers in paleontology, archaeology and ecology.

Connie Hofferber Jones

Camp Cooks

One or two cooks are hired at each facility depending on the number of people being fed. Some are school cooks or teachers with summers off, some are professional cooks who enjoy children and the relaxed atmosphere and community feeling of camp life. Cooks are sought who enjoy cooking and serving family style and baking fresh muffins for breakfast, cookies for lunch and bread for dinner.

Connie Hofferber Jones

▪ CHOCOLATE MOUSSE PIE ▪

3 cups chocolate wafer cookies, finely ground
½ cup unsalted butter, melted
1 pound semi-sweet chocolate
2 whole eggs, very fresh
4 egg yolks, very fresh
2 cups heavy cream
6 tablespoons powdered sugar
4 egg whites, at room temperature

In a large bowl, combine chocolate wafer crumbs and butter until well mixed. Press evenly into the bottom and completely up the sides of a 10-inch springform pan. Refrigerate 30 minutes.

Place semi-sweet chocolate in the top of a double-boiler and melt over simmering water. Remove from heat and cool to luke-warm. Beat in whole eggs. Add egg yolks and beat until smooth.

In a chilled bowl, beat cream to soft peaks. add powdered sugar and continue beating until stiff peaks are formed. In a separate bowl, beat egg whites until stiff. Whisk in ¼ of the whipped cream and ¼ of the egg whites into the chocolate to lighten it. Carefully fold in remaining whipped cream and egg whites until smooth.

Pour filling into prepared crust and chill for at least 6 hours. Loosen crust on all sides with a sharp knife. Remove springform pan. Serve with additional whipped cream, if desired.

Marilyn Loy

▪ PUMPKIN PIE ▪

2 cups pumpkin, cooked and strained **OR** canned plain pumpkin
1 cup milk
3 egg yolks, beaten
1 cup sugar
1¼ teaspoons cinnamon
1¼ teaspoons ginger
1 teaspoon salt
1 teaspoon vanilla
¼ teaspoon cloves
¼ teaspoon nutmeg
3 egg whites, beaten until stiff
One 9-inch unbaked pie shell

Preheat oven to 350 degrees.

In a large bowl, mix pumpkin and milk together. Add egg yolks, sugar, cinnamon, ginger, salt, vanilla, cloves and nutmeg and beat until smooth. Gently fold in beaten egg whites just until incorporated, taking care not to deflate egg whites.

Pour filling into pie shell and bake for about 45 to 50 minutes, or until a knife inserted in the center of pie filling comes out clean.

Kathy Marsh

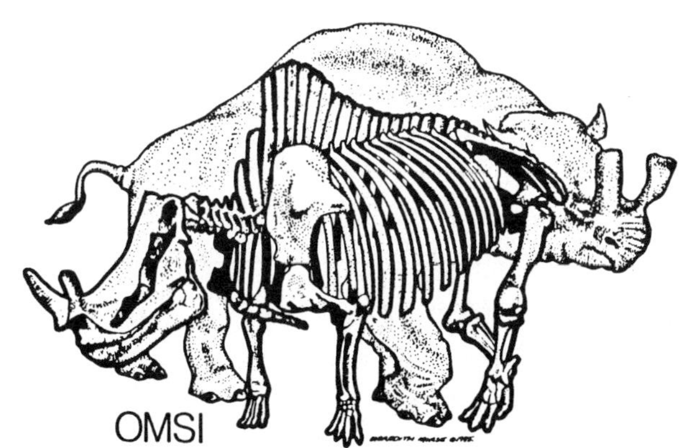

▪ TUALATIN MOUNTAIN APPLE PIE ▪

Congresswoman Elizabeth Furse is the first woman to represent Oregon's First District. A mother of two grown children, Furse and her husband, John Platt, own and operate Helvetia Vineyards, producing Pinot Noir and Chardonnay grapes in the rolling, wooded hills of the Tualatin Mountains in Washington County. In addition to the vineyards, the 80-acre farm supports a variety of apple trees, including Northern Spy, Criterion, Spartan, Spitzenburg and Jonnagold. This recipe is a family favorite.

Pie Crust:

- 2½ cups hard-wheat flour **OR** all-purpose flour
- 1 teaspoon salt
- 1 cup shortening, chilled
- 4 to 8 tablespoons ice water

Sift flour and salt into a large bowl. Make a well in the center and add shortening. Cut shortening into flour mixture with a pastry cutter until mixture resembles oatmeal. Sprinkle 4 to 8 tablespoons of water, a little at a time, over flour mixture. Add just enough water for dough to hold together. Stir gently until just moistened. Do not overmix. Gather dough into a ball and divide in half. Gently flatten into discs. Cover and chill to make rolling easier.

Filling:

- 6 to 8 medium Northern Spy **OR** Hood River Gravenstein apples, **OR** other tart apples
- ½ cup sugar
- 2 tablespoons flour
- ¾ teaspoon cinnamon
- ½ teaspoon freshly grated nutmeg **OR** 1 teaspoon ground nutmeg
- ¼ teaspoon ginger
- ¼ teaspoon salt
- 1 tablespoon lemon juice
- 2 tablespoons unsalted butter
- 1 tablespoon melted butter
- 1 tablespoon sugar

Preheat oven to 450 degrees.

Peel, core and thinly slice apples and place in large bowl. Combine ½ cup sugar, 2 tablespoons flour, cinnamon, nutmeg, ginger and salt in a small bowl and stir with a fork to blend well. Add to apples and toss to coat evenly.

On a well-floured board, roll out half of the dough and fit into a 9½-inch pie plate. Trim the edge to make a ½-inch overhang. Prick all over with a fork. Put apple mixture into pie shell. Sprinkle with lemon juice and dot with 2 tablespoons butter. Roll out remaining dough and fit over filling, trimming the edge to a 1-inch overhang. Fold top crust under bottom crust and crimp together decoratively. Make decorative slits in top crust for steam vents.

Put pie in preheated oven and immediately turn heat down to 350 degrees. Bake for 40 to 50 minutes, or until apples are tender and crust is golden brown. When done, remove from oven and immediately brush with 1 tablespoon melted butter and sprinkle with 1 tablespoon sugar.

This pie is best when served hot from the oven. Top with a thick slice of sharp Tillamook County cheddar cheese. Or top with a dollop of whipped cream, a spoonful of warmed sweet Oregon Apple Jack Brandy and sprinkle with freshly grated nutmeg.

Elizabeth Furse
Member of Congress

Camp Lunch

All groups head out to the field for four to five hours each morning and lunch is taken along in each backpack. After breakfast the cooks put out lunch materials—bread, sandwich meat and cheese, tuna fish, lettuce, sprouts, pickles, carrots and celery sticks, cookies, trail mix and fruit. Each student or camper packs his or her own variety of lunch with the quantity to match the appetite.

Connie Hofferber Jones

Camp Hancock Dining Room Duties

Campers get manners and dishwashing lessons free of charge in OMSI programs. The groups eat family style, and are encouraged to pass the food politely around the table. With counselor supervision, campers set the tables, clear them and help in washing the dishes after each meal.

Connie Hofferber Jones

▪ LEMON FROST PIE ▪

1 cup flour
2 tablespoons sugar
¼ teaspoon salt
½ cup butter
1 cup heavy cream
¼ cup lemon juice
2 teaspoon lemon zest, minced
5 drops yellow food coloring
2 egg whites, from very fresh eggs
⅔ cup sugar

Preheat the oven to 375 degrees. Lightly grease and flour a 9-inch pie plate.

In a large bowl, sift together flour, 2 tablespoons sugar and salt. Using a pastry blender or fork, cut the butter in until the mixture resembles coarse meal.

Place ⅓ cup of this mixture in a baking dish. Press the remaining mixture evenly into the prepared pie plate. Bake both for 12 to 15 minutes. Cool completely.

In a large bowl, whip the heavy cream. Fold in lemon juice, lemon zest and food coloring. Chill. In a separate bowl, beat the egg whites until they hold soft peaks. Gradually add the sugar, beating constantly until all of the sugar is incorporated and they hold stiff peaks. Carefully fold together the egg white mixture and the whipped cream mixture until smooth.

Pour filling into cooled pie shell. Sprinkle over reserved ⅓ cup cooled crumbs. Chill or freeze. Serve with Blueberry Sauce.

Blueberry Sauce:

⅔ cup sugar
1 tablespoon cornstarch
⅛ teaspoon salt
⅔ cup water
2 cups blueberries, fresh or frozen

Stir together sugar, cornstarch and salt in a medium sauce pan. Add water in a thin stream, whisking constantly until smooth. Cook over medium heat, whisking constantly, until thickened. Stir in blueberries and bring to a boil, stirring constantly. Remove from heat and chill.

Lynda Johnston

▪ FRESH PEACH PIE ▪

1½ cups fresh peaches, peeled and thinly sliced
¾ cup sugar
1 tablespoon unflavored gelatin
¼ cup cold water
½ cup boiling water
1 tablespoon fresh lemon juice
¼ teaspoon salt
½ cup heavy cream
One 9-inch pre-baked pie shell

In a medium bowl, combine peaches and sugar and let stand for 30 minutes. In a large bowl, soften gelatin in ¼ cup cold water for 10 minutes. Stir in boiling water. Let mixture cool, stirring often. Add peach mixture, lemon juice and salt and mix thoroughly. Chill in the refrigerator for about 30 minutes, stirring occasionally, until slightly thickened.

Whip cream until firm peaks are formed. Carefully fold whipped cream into the peach mixture until smooth, taking care not to deflate the whipped cream. Pour mixture into baked pie shell and chill at least 6 hours, or overnight, before serving.

Patti Babler

▪ COLIN'S APPLE PIE ▪

When I created this recipe, I was determined to come up with a new version of apple pie, different from any I'd seen, and as "apple-y" as I could make it. (I believe I kept muttering something like, "I'm going to make the best damn apple pie I possibly can!") Esplanade customers and I have been very happy with the results. As so many are, this pie is very tasty served warm with a scoop of good vanilla ice cream. It's also excellent with a slice of extra-sharp cheddar cheese---anything less than extra-sharp is lost against the intense apple flavor. In spite of the lengthy instructions, this pie is really very easy to make.

Orange-Cornmeal Shortbread Crust:

1 cup unsalted butter, at room temperature
⅔ cup sugar
Zest from 1 orange, finely minced
1⅔ cups flour, sifted before measuring
½ cup yellow cornmeal
¼ cup rice flour
2 egg whites, beaten until foamy

Northwest Apple Pie Filling:

½ cup apple juice
5 teaspoons Clear Creek Apple Brandy (or any brand of apple brandy or applejack)
⅓ cup sugar
5 tablespoons apple juice
¼ cup cornstarch
½ cup sugar
2½ tablespoons unsalted butter
3¾ teaspoons fresh lemon juice
½ teaspoon salt
2 pounds tart green cooking apples, such as Washington State Pippins (approximately 6 medium apples)
½ cup dry bread crumbs

Streusel Topping:

1¼ cups flour
10 tablespoons brown sugar
¼ cup sugar
¼ teaspoon cinnamon
⅛ teaspoon mace
⅛ teaspoon salt
6 tablespoons unsalted butter, at room temperature

Preheat oven to 375 degrees.

For the Orange-Cornmeal Shortbread Crust: Cream the butter and sugar together until very light and creamy, about 10 minutes. When ready, the butter should be nearly white in color. Stir in orange zest.

Sift together the 1⅔ cups flour, cornmeal and rice flour and add to the creamed mixture. Mix on low speed until just combined.

Remove the bottom of an ungreased 10-inch by 2-inch springform pan. Take two-thirds of the shortbread mixture and pat it into place on the pan bottom. With a rolling pin, roll over the dough on the pan bottom to level out the dough and trim off any excess. Place dough-lined bottom into the springform "ring" and secure the "ring" in place. Take remaining shortbread dough and press it into place inside the springform "ring". (This is best accomplished by rolling the dough into a length of "rope" and fitting it inside the ring, then flattening the dough.) Dough should line the side of the pan nearly to the top. Use fingers to press dough firmly into place where the side of the pan joins the bottom, so there will be no crack. Refrigerate the dough-lined pan for 20 minutes, or until thoroughly chilled.

Line dough with foil and fill with dried beans or pie weights. Bake for about 15 minutes, or until sides of crust is golden brown. Remove from oven and remove foil and beans. Return to oven and bake an additional 15 minutes or until bottom crust is golden brown. Remove from oven and brush hot crust with beaten egg whites. (This will seal the crust and help it from becoming soggy when filling is added.) Return to oven and bake for 1 minute to cook egg whites. Remove from oven and cool slightly.

For the Northwest Apple Pie Filling:

In a medium sauce pan, combine ½ cup apple juice, Apple Brandy and ⅓ cup sugar, and whisk until sugar is dissolved. In a small bowl, combine 5 tablespoons apple juice and cornstarch and whisk until smooth. Whisk cornstarch mixture into mixture in pan. Bring to a boil over medium heat, stirring constantly. Cook for 1 minute then remove from heat.

Combine ½ cup sugar, butter, lemon juice and salt. Stir into cooked juice mixture until sugar and butter are dissolved. Stir mixture into sliced apples.

For the Streusel Topping:

In a medium bowl, stir together 1¼ cups flour, brown sugar, ¼ cup sugar, cinnamon, mace and salt. Add 6 tablespoons butter and mix by hand, or with a mixer on low speed, until crumbly.

Assembly:

With a paring knife, trim baked shortbread crust 1-inch from top of springform pan. Discard scraps. Sprinkle dry bread crumbs evenly across bottom of baked crust. Place apple filling in crust, spreading it evenly into place, so filling is level with top of crust.

Bake at 375 degrees for 40 minutes, or until filling starts to bubble at edges. Remove pie from oven and pat streusel topping evenly on top of filling. Return pie to oven and bake for an additional 10 to 15 minutes, or until streusel topping is golden brown.

Remove from oven and cool. When pie is cool, remove sides from springform pan. With a metal spatula or large knife, carefully loosen pie from bottom of springform pan. Gently slide onto serving platter. Serves 10.

Colin Cameron
RiverPlace Hotel
Portland, Oregon

▪ EINSTEIN PI (CHERRY PIE) ▪

Albert Einstein's birthday is March 14, or 3.14. . . pi, more or less. His favorite meal was Chicken and Dumplings (page 66) and Cherry Pie. Serve this to celebrate his birthday.

Cherry Filling:

1 quart sour cherries, pitted
1 cup sugar
2 tablespoons cornstarch
4 tablespoons butter

Preheat oven to 425 degrees.

Place pitted cherries in a large bowl. Mix together sugar and cornstarch with a fork and toss with the cherries. Pour cherry mixture into a 10-inch unbaked pie shell and dot with butter. Top with a lattice crust and flute the edges. Bake at 425 degrees for 10 minutes. Reduce heat to 350 degrees and bake an additional 40 minutes.

Pie Crust:

5 cups flour
1 cup butter
1 cup shortening
½ cup cold water
1 egg
1 tablespoon lemon juice
1 tablespoon sugar
1¼ teaspoon baking powder
1 teaspoon salt

In a large bowl combine flour, butter and shortening until mixture resembles oatmeal. In a separate bowl combine remaining ingredients and stir with fork until smooth.

Pour liquid over flour mixture and stir gently until just moistened. Do not overmix. Gather dough into ball and divide into thirds. Gently flatten into discs. Cover and chill to make rolling easier. Makes enough dough for one double-crust pie and one single-crust pie.

Martha Lunde Hovey
Leslie J. Whipple

▪ PERFECT APPLE PIE ▪

Pie Filling:

2½ pounds tart green apples, (about 3 large Granny Smith, Pippin or Newton apples)
½ cup sugar
3 tablespoons flour
2 teaspoons cinnamon
⅓ cup honey
2 tablespoons fresh lemon juice
1 10-inch unbaked pie shell

Crumb Topping:

½ cup flour
⅓ cup sugar
1 teaspoon cinnamon
4 tablespoons butter, melted

Preheat oven to 375 degrees.

For the Filling:

In a large bowl, combine ½ cup sugar, 3 tablespoons flour and 2 teaspoons cinnamon and set aside. Peel, core, and thinly slice apples. Add to sugar mixture and toss to coat. Add honey and lemon juice and stir until apple slices are well coated and syrupy. Pour into unbaked pie shell.

For the Topping:

In a medium bowl, combine ½ cup flour, ⅓ cup sugar and 1 teaspoon cinnamon. Add melted butter and stir until large crumbs are formed. Sprinkle over apples . Place pie on baking sheet to protect oven from spills and cover pie crust rim with a foil collar. Bake for about 50 minutes, or until topping is golden brown and filling is beginning to bubble.

Sylvia Gere Emard

Food Waste

At Hancock Field Station garbage is separated for recycling, including the food waste, which is handled by the field station's four pigs. At all the camps, minimizing food waste is emphasized with skits and reward systems. A group of 60 often can reduce the food left on all the plates to less than one pound per meal.

Connie Hofferber Jones

▪ BLACKBERRY CREAM PIE ▪

1 8-ounce package cream cheese, at room temperature
3 tablespoons sugar
1 teaspoon vanilla
1 cup whipping cream
½ cup sugar
2 tablespoons cornstarch
¼ cup water
3 pints fresh blackberries
1 10-inch pre-baked pie shell

In a large bowl, combine cream cheese with 3 tablespoons sugar and vanilla and beat until smooth. Slowly blend in cream and mix until very smooth. Pour mixture into prebaked pie shell and chill.

In a medium saucepan, stir together ½ cup sugar and cornstarch. Add water and 1 pint of the blackberries. Cook, stirring constantly, over medium heat until mixture is thick and smooth. Remove from heat and force through a sieve to strain out seeds. When cool, spread thickened blackberry mixture over cream cheese mixture in pie shell.

Press remaining 2 pints whole blackberries into pie filling in concentric circles. Chill at least 4 hours before serving.

Sylvia Gere Emard

▪ BOURBON AND WALNUT PIE ▪

I used to make this pie at Pat & Mike's Cinema/Restaurant in Bend, Oregon many years ago. It was very popular, but I discontinued making it because I couldn't keep bourbon in the restaurant kitchen. I went in about 5 AM to bake desserts and the bourbon bottle was always empty, no matter how often it was replaced. We decided that it wasn't cost-effective!

$2\frac{1}{2}$ cups dark corn syrup
2 tablespoons bourbon
$\frac{1}{2}$ cup butter, melted and cooled
2 eggs
$\frac{1}{4}$ teaspoon salt
$2\frac{1}{2}$ cups chopped walnuts
1 10-inch unbaked pie shell

Preheat oven to 350 degrees.

In a large bowl, blend together corn syrup, bourbon and melted butter. Beat in eggs and salt. Stir in chopped walnuts and pour into pie shell. Bake for about 40 to 50 minutes, or until filling is just set. Cool completely before serving.

Sylvia Gere Emard

▪ LIME SLICES ▪

6 tablespoons butter
2 tablespoons sugar
$\frac{3}{4}$ cup flour
$\frac{1}{3}$ cup cornstarch
1 14-ounce can sweetened condensed milk
2 egg yolks
$\frac{1}{2}$ cup fresh lime juice
2 teaspoons lime zest
1 drop green food coloring (optional)
2 egg whites
$\frac{1}{4}$ cup sugar
1 cup sweetened coconut, divided in half

Preheat oven to 375 degrees. Grease an 11-inch by 7-inch by $1\frac{1}{2}$-inch baking dish. Line bottom with parchment paper and grease parchment.

In a large bowl, cream together butter and 2 tablespoons sugar until smooth. Sift together flour and cornstarch. Add to creamed mixture slowly, beating constantly. Mixture will be crumbly. Turn dough out onto lightly floured surface and knead for 5 minutes. Spread dough evenly into prepared baking dish. Bake for 15 minutes, or until lightly browned.

In a large bowl, combine condensed milk, egg yolks, lime juice, lime zest and food coloring and blend well. Pour lime mixture over partially baked crust and return to oven. Bake 10 minutes.

In a large bowl, beat egg whites until soft peaks are formed. Gradually add $\frac{1}{4}$ cup sugar and beat until sugar is dissolved. Fold in half of the coconut. Spread egg white mixture evenly over partially cooked lime mixture. Sprinkle remaining $\frac{1}{2}$ cup coconut over the top. Return to the oven and bake an additional 10 minutes, or until golden brown.

Cool completely before cutting. Serve at room temperature or chilled. Store in the refrigerator. Yield: 16 slices.

Jim and Karen Bosley

▪ ORANGE RICOTTA TARTLETTES ▪

1 pound ricotta
½ cup sugar
2 egg yolks
1 tablespoon fresh orange juice
2 teaspoons orange zest, finely minced
½ teaspoon orange flower water
½ teaspoon vanilla
⅛ teaspoon cinnamon
⅛ teaspoon salt
1 pound puff pastry

Preheat oven to 375 degrees.

In a large bowl, combine ricotta, sugar, egg yolks, orange juice, zest, orange flower water, vanilla, cinnamon and salt and beat until well mixed. Cut puff pastry into 3-inch squares and press into muffin tins. Place filling in the center and bake for about 20 minutes, or until pastry is golden and filling is set.

Or cut pastry into 6-inch squares and place on baking sheet. Place filling in the center and fold in half diagonally to form a triangle. Seal edges together with a little water and bake until golden.

Leslie J. Whipple

▪ CINNAMON AND RAISIN PUFF ▪

Crust:

1 cup flour
¼ cup sugar
½ cup butter
2 tablespoons cold water

Filling:

2 tablespoons sugar
¾ cup brown sugar
1½ cups raisins
1 teaspoon cinnamon
3 tablespoons sugar

Custard:

1 cup water
½ cup butter
¼ cup sugar
1 teaspoon vanilla
1 cup flour
3 eggs

Topping:

1½ cups powdered sugar
2 teaspoons butter, softened
1½ teaspoons vanilla
1 to 2 tablespoons hot water
¼ cup walnuts, finely chopped

Preheat oven to 350 degrees.

For the Crust:

In a large bowl, combine 1 cup flour and ¼ cup sugar. Cut in the ½ cup butter until the mixture resembles coarse meal. Sprinkle 2 tablespoons cold water over and combine just until the dough holds together. Place dough on a pizza pan. Flour your hands and pat dough out to about a 12-inch circle. Pinch the edges decoratively.

For the Filling:

Sprinkle filling ingredients, in order they are given, over the crust. Press gently into the crust. Refrigerate until needed.

For the Custard:

Place 1 cup water, ½ cup butter and ¼ cup sugar in a sauce pan. Bring to a simmer over low heat until sugar dissolves. Increase heat to high and bring to a boil. Remove from heat and beat in 1 teaspoon vanilla and 1 cup flour until mixture pulls away from the sides of the sauce pan and forms a ball. Beat in the eggs until mixture is smooth and glossy. Spread custard mixture completely over the sugar and raisin topping, and seal to the edge of the crust. Bake for about 45 minutes or until topping is golden brown. The custard will puff up and then fall. Remove from oven and let cool.

For the Topping:

Combine powdered sugar, butter, vanilla and hot water and stir until smooth. Drizzle over cooled custard. Sprinkle the walnuts over the top. Cut into thin wedges and enjoy.

Rhonda J. Grishaw

▪ GOLDEN APRICOT AND PINEAPPLE PITA ▪

A VIENNESE PASTRY

My Auntie, Veronika Spring and her husband Krischtof, came to Portland, Oregon in 1911 from Austria-Hungary. She was just a bride. She brought many of her recipes from home. This Pita was one of the families' favorites, especially at Christmas. She would pile them high on a large white platter and they would disappear quickly. Veronika and Krischtof Spring operated their home Viennese Pastry shop on N.E. Hassalo Street for many years. The shop has long been gone, but her recipes are still with us to enjoy.

Pastry:

4 cups flour
¼ teaspoon salt
1 pound butter, very cold
3 egg yolks
Zest of 1 lemon, finely minced

Filling:

1½ cups apricot-pineapple jam
3 large apples, peeled and grated
(if apples are very juicy, drain on paper towels)

Topping:

3 egg whites, beaten until foamy
1½ cups finely ground walnuts
3 tablespoons sugar

Preheat oven to 350 degrees.

Stir flour and salt together in a large bowl. Cut in butter quickly, using a pastry cutter or fork, until mixture resembles coarse meal. Make a well in the center and add egg yolks and lemon zest. Mix with a wooden spoon until dough just holds together. Gather dough into a ball and divide in half. Refrigerate half of the dough. Turn half the dough out onto a well floured board and roll out into a rectangle that will fit inside an 18-inch by 12-inch by 1-inch jelly roll pan. Carefully place dough into pan and prick all over with a fork.

Spread dough with apricot-pineapple jam. Arrange apple slices over jam and refrigerate until needed.

Roll out other half of dough and carefully place it onto first half of dough, so now filling is sandwiched in between dough. Brush top of dough with egg whites. Sprinkle evenly with walnuts. Sprinkle sugar over walnuts.

Bake for 25 to 30 minutes, or until pastry is cooked through. Cool in pan, then cut in squares to serve.

Sandra Greening

▪ NANA'S QUICK COBBLER ▪

Nana always put her cobbler into the oven as she pulled out the dinner biscuits so we would have hot cobbler for desert. She told me that her mother taught her to make this when she was a young girl, circa 1920s, in the Oklahoma territory. Nana taught me to make this when I was a young girl in the 1960s.

1 cup flour
1 cup sugar
2 teaspoons baking powder
1 teaspoon salt
⅔ cup milk
½ cup butter
1 1-pound can of cherries, peaches or fruit cocktail

Preheat oven to 425 degrees.

In a large bowl, combine flour, sugar, baking powder and salt. Add milk and blend well. Cut butter into 8 pieces and place on the bottom of a glass 8-inch square baking dish. Pour batter over butter. Pour fruit over batter. Bake for 10 minutes then reduce heat to 325 degrees and bake for about 45 minutes, or until top is golden brown. Serves 6 to 8.

Bridget Smith

▪ OUTRAGEOUS OLALLIEBERRY PASTRY ▪

Olallieberry jam is from a newer variety of berry that was created some forty years ago and named Olallie, the name by which the Columbia River Chinook Indians called all "black" berries. George Waldo, of the U.S. Department of Agriculture, Corvallis, Oregon, developed the berry by crossing a Black Loganberry with a Youngberry. This jam's flavor and fragrance are unforgettable. It is our favorite, and one to be tried.

This is a simple yet elegant pastry!

2 cups flour
½ teaspoon salt
1 cup butter
1 cup sour cream
12 ounces Morin's Landing Olallieberry Jam **OR** Morin's Landing Sugarless Olallieberry Jam
1 cup shredded coconut
½ cup powdered sugar, optional

Preheat oven to 350 degrees. Grease 2 baking sheets.

Sift flour and salt together into a large bowl. Cut in butter with a pastry blender until the mixture resembles coarse meal. Mix in sour cream. Refrigerate overnight.

Remove dough from refrigerator and let stand at room temperature for 1 hour. Divide dough in half. Turn dough out onto a lightly floured surface and roll out to 10-inch by 15-inch rectangle. Spread with half the Olallieberry Jam and sprinkle with half of the coconut. Roll up jelly-roll style, beginning with the long edge. Repeat with remaining ingredients.

Place each roll on prepared baking sheets and bake for 45 minutes. Cool, then sprinkle with powdered sugar. Slice and serve. Serves 18.

Joyce Bolliger
Morin's Landing

▪ RHUBARB CRISP ▪

4 cups fresh rhubarb, cut into 1-inch pieces
1 cup sugar
½ cup water
¼ cup flour
½ teaspoon cinnamon
¾ cup flour
1 cup brown sugar
½ cup quick-cooking oatmeal
½ cup melted butter

Preheat oven to 350 degrees. Grease an 8-inch by 8-inch baking pan.

Put prepared rhubarb in a large bowl. In a small bowl combine 1 cup sugar, water, ¼ cup flour and cinnamon and mix with a fork. Pour over rhubarb and stir to combine. Pour into prepared baking dish.

In a medium bowl, stir together ¾ cup flour, brown sugar and oatmeal until well mixed. Stir in melted butter. Sprinkle oatmeal mixture evenly over rhubarb mixture in pan. Bake for about 35 minutes, or until rhubarb is tender and topping is golden brown.

Patti Babler

Camp Food

For people hiking five hours a day, swimming an hour, and being outside all day long in the chilly spring and fall or the hot summer, fueling them is a vital part of the program. Camp food at OMSI camps is not just hot dogs and hamburgers. Nutritious, balanced and enjoyable meals are required. Stews, spaghetti, enchiladas, fried rice, baked chicken, lasagna with freshly baked bread, a vegetable and a salad are some of the evening meals. Pancakes, French toast, scrambled eggs, hard boiled eggs and muffins provide hearty breakfasts.

Connie Hofferber Jones

▪ CRUNCHY BITS ▪

3 cups blueberries, rinsed and drained
⅔ cup brown sugar
½ cup flour
¼ cup butter
¼ teaspoon nutmeg
¼ teaspoon salt
⅔ cup quick-cooking oatmeal

Preheat oven to 400 degrees. Lightly grease an 8-inch by 8-inch baking dish.

Place blueberries in baking dish and set aside.

In a large bowl, combine brown sugar, flour, butter, nutmeg and salt and mix with a fork until mixture is crumbly. Stir in oatmeal. Spread mixture evenly over blueberries. Bake for 20 minutes, or until topping is crisp and brown.

Wendy Whitsell

▪ THE ULTIMATE RASPBERRY COBBLER ▪

This is my mother-in-law's recipe, and the best cobbler I've ever had---and everyone who's tasted it seems to agree. I think the brown sugar and buttermilk are the secret, which makes it taste sweet and slightly crunchy. I prefer frozen raspberries because they are so easy and slightly tarter.

Filling:

2 pints raspberries **OR** 2 small bags frozen (thawed)
¾ cup sugar
1½ tablespoons flour

Topping:

1 cup flour
½ cup sugar
½ cup brown sugar
½ teaspoon baking powder
⅛ teaspoon salt
½ cup melted margarine **OR** butter
¼ cup buttermilk

Preheat oven to 350 degrees. Grease and flour a rectangle glass baking dish.

For the filling:

Stir together the ¾ cup sugar and 1½ tablespoons flour and toss with the raspberries. Place in the bottom of prepared baking dish.

For the topping:

In a large bowl, stir together 1 cup flour, ½ cup sugar, brown sugar, baking powder and salt. Pour in melted margarine and buttermilk. Beat until smooth. It will look like thin cookie dough. Drop by large spoonfuls onto filling. Spread slightly but leave spots of filling peeping through.

Bake for about 45 minutes, or until crust is golden brown. Top with whipped cream or vanilla ice cream.

Bridget R. Wise

▪ RHUBARB AND PECAN CRISP ▪

1 cup flour
½ cup sugar
½ teaspoon salt
1 cup oatmeal
½ cup pecans, chopped
½ cup melted butter
3 cups rhubarb, sliced into ½-inch pieces
½ teaspoon water
½ cup sugar
1 tablespoon flour
½ teaspoon cinnamon

Preheat oven to 350 degrees. Grease a 9-inch pie plate.

In a large bowl, sift together 1 cup flour, ½ cup sugar and salt. Stir in the oatmeal and pecans. Add melted butter and mix until crumbly. Press half of the mixture into prepared pie plate. Reserve the other half of the mixture for the topping.

Place rhubarb in a large bowl and sprinkle with water. Combine ½ cup sugar, 1 tablespoon flour and cinnamon in a small bowl and stir with a fork to mix. Pour mixture over rhubarb and toss to coat evenly. Place rhubarb mixture over bottom crust in pie plate and sprinkle reserved topping mixture evenly over rhubarb. Bake for about 45 minutes, or until crust is light brown and rhubarb is tender.

Anjelle Ruppe

COOKIES

▪ THE OMSI VOLUNTEER PROGRAM ▪

The Science of Sharing

OMSI's tradition with volunteers extends to the museum's very beginning. Volunteers literally built OMSI and that tradition continues today. When OMSI outgrew it's home on NE Hassalo Street, the Board of Directors set out to build a bigger and better museum at Washington Park. One hot August day in 1957, six hundred volunteer bricklayers and hod carriers gathered at the site to build the outside walls in a day. Volunteers continue to help us build our museum, perhaps not by laying actual bricks, but by sharing their enthusiasm and excitement about OMSI with the public.

The volunteer program has several options in which people may share their time. The actual day to day operation of the museum requires about 300 volunteers weekly. There volunteers make a long term commitment of three months or more, generally volunteering for one four hour shift per week. In-museum volunteers serve OMSI as Greeters welcoming visitors to the museum, or as Explorers on the Exhibit floor making science come alive for our visitors. They assist in the store, the mailroom, or as theater ushers. Some volunteers work behind the scenes planning activities and events for community programs. These volunteers participate in a comprehensive orientation and training program familiarizing themselves with OMSI and the OMSI style of "hands on" science.

Some volunteers, in fact around five to six hundred, assist us throughout the year on fund raising projects such as the OMSI Auction, Epicurean Experience, Winter Solstice and Phonathon. Others share their expertise and talents with special programs or events. These volunteers generally assist during the planning or actual day of the event for fairly short term assignments. Other volunteers serve on the Board of Directors or the OMSI Council in fund raising and advisory capacities.

The volunteer program continues to grow and evolve as people bring their particular skills and expertise to the museum to share. Volunteers are always needed and through the interview process we make every effort to match a volunteer's skills and enthusiasm to a need in the museum. Volunteers are assured of having fun and of knowing they've made a difference when they decide to participate in the Science of Sharing.

Marcia Hale
Manager Volunteer Services

▪ RUSSIAN TEACAKES ▪

1 cup butter, at room temperature
½ cup powdered sugar
1 teaspoon vanilla
2¼ cups flour
⅛ teaspoon salt
¾ cup finely ground walnuts
Powdered sugar

Preheat oven to 400 degrees.

In a large bowl, beat together butter, ½ cup powdered sugar and vanilla until light and fluffy. Add flour, salt and walnuts and mix until smooth and dough holds together.

Shape dough into balls the size of a walnut. Place 1-inch apart on ungreased baking sheets. Bake just until set but not brown, about 10 to 12 minutes. Roll in powdered sugar while warm. Cool. Roll in powdered sugar again.

Ann Marie Adams

▪ GRANOLA BARS ▪

3 cups quick-cooking oatmeal
1 cup shredded coconut
1 cup raisins
1 cup salted sunflower seeds
1½ teaspoons cinnamon
1 14-ounce can sweetened condensed milk
½ cup melted butter

Preheat oven to 325 degrees. Line a 15-inch by 10-inch jelly roll pan with foil and spray with vegetable oil spray.

In a large bowl, combine oatmeal, coconut, raisins, sunflower seeds and cinnamon and stir to mix. Combine sweetened condensed milk and melted butter and stir into oatmeal mixture until well blended. Pat mixture evenly into prepared pan and bake 25 to 30 minutes, or until lightly browned. Cool slightly. Cut into 50 bars. Great snacks for hiking and backpacking.

Carolyn Rose

Caffeine makes its way to the cortex of the brain about 30 minutes after it's consumed and continues to stimulate the nervous system for up to eight hours afterward.

▪ ORANGE COOKIES ▪

Orange Cookies:

½ cup sugar
3 tablespoons margarine OR butter
3 tablespoons shortening
1 egg
⅓ cup buttermilk
2 tablespoons orange juice
2 teaspoons orange zest, finely minced
1⅓ cups flour
½ teaspoon baking powder
¼ teaspoon baking soda

Orange Frosting:

2 cups powdered sugar
3 tablespoons orange juice
3 tablespoons orange zest, finely minced

Preheat oven to 350 degrees.

For the Orange Cookies:

In a large bowl cream together sugar, margarine and shortening. Add egg and beat until light and fluffy. Stir in buttermilk, 3 tablespoons orange juice and 2 teaspoons orange zest until blended. Sift together flour, baking powder and baking soda and add to creamed mixture. Beat until well combined. Drop by teaspoonful onto ungreased baking sheets. Bake for 10 to 13 minutes. Remove cookies to a rack. Cool completely then frost. Makes 2 dozen.

For the Orange Frosting:

In a medium bowl, beat together powdered sugar, 3 tablespoons orange juice and 3 tablespoons orange zest until smooth.

Toni J. Ives

▪ JENNIFER'S SOFT AND CHEWY CHOCOLATE CHIP COOKIES ▪

1 cup butter
1 cup brown sugar
1 cup sugar
2 large eggs
1 tablespoon milk
1 tablespoon vanilla
3 cups flour*
1 teaspoon baking soda
1 teaspoon salt
1 cup milk chocolate chips, or semi-sweet chocolate chips
½ cups walnuts, chopped

Preheat oven to 350 degrees.

In a large bowl, cream together butter, brown sugar, sugar and eggs until smooth. Beat in milk and vanilla. Sift flour, baking soda and salt into mixture in bowl and blend well. Stir in chocolate chips and walnuts. Drop by large teaspoonfuls onto cookie sheets and bake for about 8 to 10 minutes. Cool just a little and enjoy.

* I use 2 cups all-purpose flour and 1 cup whole wheat flour.

Jennifer Jenkins

▪ BEST IN THE UNIVERSE OATMEAL DATE COOKIES ▪

1 cup dates, chopped
1 cup raisins, chopped
1 cup water
¾ cup shortening
½ cup brown sugar
¼ cup buttermilk
2 eggs
1 teaspoon vanilla
1 cup flour
1 teaspoon cinnamon
½ teaspoon baking soda
¼ teaspoon baking powder
3 cups oatmeal

Preheat oven to 350 degrees.

In a small sauce pan, combine dates, raisins and water and simmer over medium-low heat until soft. Cool completely.

In a large bowl, cream together shortening and brown sugar until light and fluffy. Add buttermilk, eggs and vanilla and beat until smooth. Stir in date mixture.

Sift together flour, cinnamon, baking soda and baking powder and beat into mixture. Mix in oatmeal until blended. Drop by spoonfuls onto baking sheets. Bake for 12 to 15 minutes. Cool on a rack.

Vernice Roberts

▪ RANGER COOKIES ▪

1 cup shortening
1 cup sugar
1 cup brown sugar
2 eggs
1 teaspoon vanilla
2 cups quick-cooking oatmeal
2 cups Rice Krispie cereal
1 cup coconut, flaked and sweetened
2 cups flour
1 teaspoon baking soda
½ teaspoon baking powder
½ teaspoon salt

Preheat oven to 350 degrees.

In a large bowl, cream together shortening, sugar and brown sugar until light and fluffy. Beat in eggs and vanilla until smooth. Stir in oatmeal, cereal and coconut. Sift together flour, baking soda, baking powder and salt and add to mixture. Stir until well blended. Form dough into balls the size of a walnut and place on ungreased baking sheets. Flatten slightly with a fork. Bake for 8 to 10 minutes. Cool on a rack.

Charles W. Manke

Apples and pears were first cultivated in Europe and Western Asia.

Major Divisions of Geologic Time

The major divisions, with brief explanations of each, are shown in the following scale of relative time, which is arranged in chronological order with the oldest division at the bottom, the youngest at the top.

CENOZOIC ERA (Age of Recent Life)	Quaternary Period	1.6 million years ago	The several geologic eras were originally named Primary, Secondary, Tertiary, and Quaternary. The first two names are no longer used; Tertiary and Quaternary have been retained but used as period designations.
	Tertiary Period	66 million years ago	
MESOZOIC ERA (Age of Medieval Life)	Cretaceous Period	138 million years ago	Derived from Latin word for chalk (creta) and first applied to extensive deposits that form white cliffs along the English Channel.
	Jurassic Period	205 million years ago	Named for the Jura Mountains, located between France and Switzerland, where rocks of this age were first studied.
	Triassic Period	240 million years ago	Taken from the word "trias" in recognition of the threefold character of these rocks in Europe.
PALEOZOIC ERA (Age of Ancient Life)	Permian Period	290 million years ago	Named after the province of Perm, U.S.S.R., where these rocks were first studied.
	Pennsylvanian Period	330 million years ago	Named for the State of Pennsylvania where these rocks have produced much coal.
	Mississippian Period	360 million years ago	Named for the Mississippi River valley where these rocks are well exposed.
	Devonian Period	410 million years ago	Named after Devonshire, England, where these rocks were first studied.
	Silurian Period	435 million years ago	Named after Celtic tribes, the Silures and the Ordovices, that lived in Wales during the Roman Conquest.
	Ordovician Period	500 million years ago	
	Cambrian Period	570 million years ago	Taken from Roman name for Wales (Cambria) where rocks containing the earliest evidence of complex forms of life were first studied.
PRECAMBRIAN			The time between the birth of the planet and the appearance of complex forms of life. More than 80 percent of the Earth's estimated 4½ billion years falls within this era.

▪ PEANUT BUTTER COOKIES ▪

I began making these cookies when I was a child in 1953. For the past 20 years we have flattened the cookies with an old family potato masher from the early 1900s. The masher is round with cut-outs, and makes a beautiful decoration on the cookies. These cookies have pleased many harvest crews on our wheat ranch in central Oregon.

1 cup shortening
1 cup sugar
1 cup brown sugar
2 eggs, beaten
1 cup peanut butter, creamy or chunky
1 teaspoon vanilla
3 cups flour
2 teaspoons baking soda
⅛ teaspoon salt

Preheat oven to 375 degrees.

In a large bowl, cream together the shortening, sugar and brown sugar until light and fluffy. Add eggs and beat until well mixed. Beat in peanut butter and vanilla. In a separate bowl sift together flour, baking soda and salt. Add flour mixture, a little at a time, to the creamed mixture and blend well. Form dough into balls the size of walnuts and place on cookie sheets. Flatten each with the tines of a fork, making a criss-cross design. Bake for 8 to 10 minutes. Cool on a rack.

Donna L. Kaseberg

▪ BUTTERMILK CINNAMON BARS ▪

I won a champion ribbon for this recipe at 4-H competition in 1973.

2 cups flour
1¼ cups sugar
¾ cup brown sugar
½ cup butter, softened
½ cup flaked coconut
½ cup chopped nuts
1 cup buttermilk
1 egg, well beaten
1 teaspoon baking powder
1 teaspoon cinnamon
1 teaspoon vanilla
½ teaspoon salt

Glaze:
1 cup powdered sugar
1 tablespoon hot water

Preheat oven to 350 degrees. Grease a 9-inch by 13-inch baking pan.

In a large bowl, stir together flour, sugar and brown sugar until blended. Add butter and cut in with a pastry blender or fork until mixture resembles coarse meal. Combine 2 cups of this mixture with coconut and nuts. Press coconut mixture into bottom of prepared pan. Set aside.

In a small bowl, combine buttermilk, egg, baking powder, cinnamon, vanilla and salt. Add to the remaining sugar and flour mixture and mix well. Spread over mixture in pan. Bake for about 45 minutes. Remove from oven and while still warm, frost with Glaze. Cut into bars.

For the Glaze:

Combine powdered sugar and water and stir until smooth.

Kim Kaseberg Decker

▪ T V BROWNIES ▪

1 cup sugar
¾ cup flour
⅓ cup cocoa powder
½ cup melted margarine **OR** butter
2 eggs
½ cup chopped nuts, (optional)

Preheat oven to 350 degrees. Grease a 9-inch by 9-inch baking pan.

In a large bowl, combine all ingredients and beat until well blended. Pour into prepared pan and bake for about 20 minutes, or just until toothpick inserted in the center comes out clean.

Senator Bob Packwood

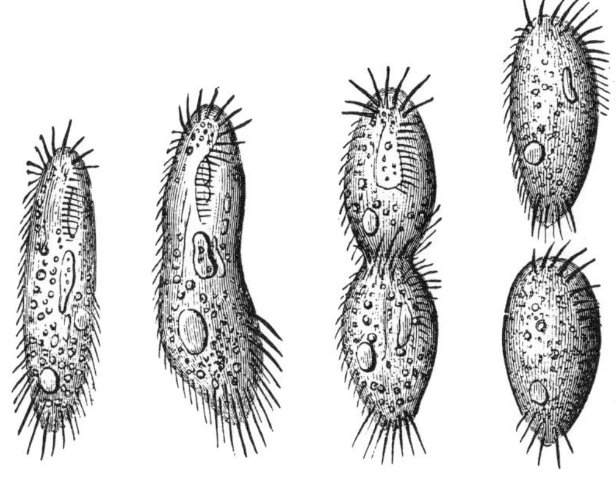

DESSERTS

▪ Winter Solstice Renaissance Festival ▪

The Renaissance Age. Those words conjure up images of artists creating masterpieces in marble and in paint; of learned men debating the accepted view of the universe; of explorers circumnavigating the globe and bringing back treasures from very foreign lands.

So many facets of our present culture are a result of the discoveries in the sciences and the arts which were a part of this awakening period of the mind in Western Europe.

OMSI celebrates the Age of the Renaissance every December. The annual Winter Solstice Renaissance Festival has become a tradition in many families. The Museum comes alive with the people and the living history of this influential period in time.

The month long festival has many aspects to it:

> A crafts faire village sits within the castle walls of the Changing Exhibit Hall. Here a visitor can wander past the stalls of many distinguished artisans from the Northwest. Each crafts person tells the tale of their specific art and its place in history, and has items within all price ranges for purchase.
>
> Next you will find, tucked among the craft stalls, characters from the past talking about the science history of cartography, the camera obscura, the principles of paint making, the art of calligraphy, the chemistry of bread baking, and other such subjects.
>
> Upon entering the Great Hall you may discover a performance of a human chess game, or a lutenist, or a band of jugglers, or a puppetry performance. Some of the festival weekends have tournaments of armored knights in battle for the honor of their royal courts.
>
> Within the cobblestone streets outside, you can examine exhibits on Leonardo Da Vinci's models of inventions that were ahead of their time, and speak with the man himself, as OMSI recreates this artist-genius.
>
> The Winter Solstice Renaissance Festival would not be complete without a simple celebration of the "return of the light" on Winter Solstice Night, December 21st. With traditions dating back centuries, the longest night of the year is recognized in song, verse, and ceremony, ending with a communal bonfire on the banks of the river to bring light into the darkest of nights.

The Traditions of the month of December are enhanced with the opportunities that this festival of the Renaissance brings to the Museum, and to Portland.

Margie Rikert

▪ COUNTRY VANILLA ICE CREAM ▪

5 eggs, very fresh
2¼ cup sugar
5 cups extra-rich 5% milk
4 cups heavy cream
5 teaspoons vanilla
½ teaspoon salt

In the bowl of an electric mixer, beat eggs until light and foamy. Gradually beat in sugar. Continue to beat until very stiff, about 30 minutes. Add remaining ingredients and blend until smooth. Pour into an ice cream maker with a 1 gallon capacity and process according to manufacturer's directions. Makes about 1 gallon.

Claris Poppert

▪ TORTONI ICE CREAM ▪

2 cups heavy cream
1 egg, very fresh, beaten
½ cup super-fine sugar
½ teaspoon almond extract
6 coconut macaroons finely crushed
¼ cup almonds, finely chopped
Maraschino cherries, red or green, sliced in half

Place 12 cupcake papers in a muffin tin.

In a large chilled bowl, beat the cream until it starts to thicken. Add the egg, sugar and almond extract and beat until soft peaks form. Stir in the crushed macaroons. Spoon mixture into cupcake papers or ramekins. Sprinkle chopped almonds over the tops and place a maraschino cherry half on to garnish. Freeze until firm, at least 2 hours. Serve directly from freezer. Serves 12.

Clara Eberius

▪ SCHAUM TORTE ▪

This melt-in-your-mouth meringue is traditionally served with ice cream and fresh strawberries, but is also wonderful with hot fudge topping.

6 egg whites
2 cups sugar
1 teaspoon vanilla
1 teaspoon vinegar
Vanilla ice cream
Strawberries

Preheat oven to 275 degrees. Grease and flour a baking sheet.

In a large bowl, beat egg whites until they hold soft peaks. Beat in the sugar, ¼ cup at a time, and continue to beat until meringue holds stiff peaks. Beat in vanilla and vinegar.

Spoon the mixture onto prepared baking sheet and make a depression in the center. Bake for about 1 hour. Cool and store in an air-tight container. To serve, place ice cream in the center of the Schaum Torte and top with strawberries. Serves 12.

Susan Sokol Blosser
Sokol Blosser Winery

AKUTAQ
"a-koo-tuck"
(Eskimo Ice Cream)

This recipe, with variations, is from the Yupik Eskimo's of the Yukon-Delta region of Southwestern Alaska.

Traditional:

Crow berries (like blueberries)
Cloud berries (salmon berries)
Fish eggs
Seal oil
Sugar

Combine the seal oil and sugar. Stir in the berries and fish eggs.

Less Traditional:

Crow berries
Cloud berries
Shortening
Sugar

Combine the shortening and sugar. Stir in the berries. The amount of shortening can vary from just enough to hold the berries together, to enough to make it the consistency of cookie dough.

Least Traditional:

Crow berries
Cloud berries
Vegetable oil
Shortening

Toss the berries with the oil and sugar. Freezing is optional.

Jean Mass

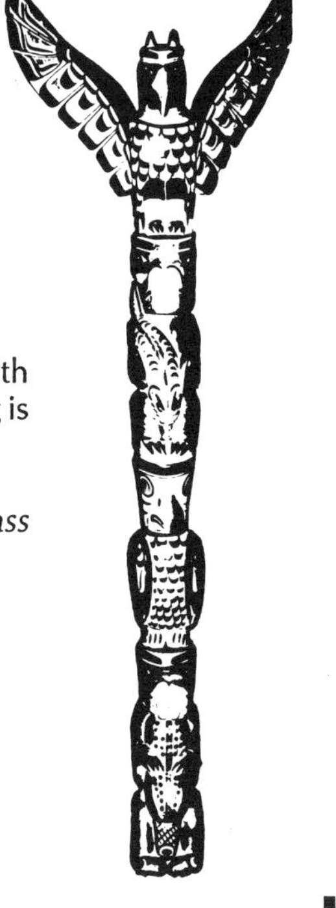

▪ FORGOTTEN DESSERT ▪

6 egg whites
1 cup sugar
½ teaspoon cream of tartar
¼ teaspoon salt
6 egg yolks
¼ cup water
⅓ cup fresh lemon juice
Zest of 1 lemon, minced
½ cup sugar
¼ teaspoon salt
2 cups heavy cream
¼ cup powdered sugar

The night before serving Forgotten Dessert, preheat oven to 425 degrees.

In a large bowl, beat egg whites until soft peaks form. Gradually beat in sugar 1 tablespoon at a time. Beat in cream of tartar and salt. Continue beating until sugar has completely dissolved and egg whites are stiff. Spread meringue in and ungreased 9-inch by 13-inch baking dish. Place in preheated oven and close the door. After exactly 1 minute, turn off the oven but do not open the door. Allow meringue to stay in the oven overnight. Do not open the oven door or the meringue will fall.

Place 6 egg yolks in a small dish and pour ¼ cup water over them. Cover with plastic wrap and refrigerate overnight.

The next day, place reserved egg yolks and ¼ cup water in the top of a double-boiler. Add lemon juice, lemon zest, sugar and salt and beat until smooth. Cook over gently simmering water, whisking constantly, until mixture is thick. Do not let mixture boil. Remove from heat and allow lemon sauce to cool.

Pour cream into a large bowl, and beat until soft peaks form. Add powdered sugar and continue beating until peaks hold their shape.

Remove meringue from oven and spread lemon sauce on top. Top with whipped cream and serve.

Corky Poppert

▪ LEMON CURD ▪

2 cups sugar
½ cup butter
Juice of 3 lemons
Zest of 3 lemons, minced
3 eggs, beaten

Place sugar, butter, lemon juice and lemon zest in the top of a double boiler, over simmering water. Whisk until sugar is dissolved. Add beaten eggs and whisk constantly until thick. Use as tart or cake filling. Store in refrigerator in airtight containers for up to 3 weeks.

Anne Amdahl

▪ SWEDISH DESSERT ▪

½ pound vanilla wafers, finely crushed
1 pound powdered sugar
½ cup butter
2 egg yolks, very fresh
2 egg whites, very fresh, beaten until stiff
1 cup crushed pineapple
½ cup maraschino cherries, chopped
⅓ cup walnuts, chopped
1 cup heavy cream
1 tablespoon sugar
1 teaspoon vanilla

Sprinkle all but ¼ cup of the vanilla wafer crumbs in the bottom of a 9-inch by 9-inch pan and set aside. In a large bowl, cream together the powdered sugar, butter and egg yolks until very light and fluffy. Gently fold in the stiffly beaten egg whites. Carefully spread this mixture over the vanilla wafer crumbs. Spread the pineapple, cherries and walnuts evenly over the creamed mixture. Whip cream until it forms soft peaks. Fold in the 1 tablespoon sugar and vanilla extract. Spread this topping over the mixture in the pan. Sprinkle the reserved ¼ cup vanilla wafer crumbs over the top. Refrigerate at least 2 hours before serving.

Shirley Curry

▪ PRALINES ▪

2 cups pecans
1½ cups sugar
1 cup light brown sugar
¾ cups evaporated milk
¼ cup light corn syrup
1 tablespoon butter
1 teaspoon vanilla

In a heavy sauce pan, mix together pecans, sugar, brown sugar, evaporated milk and corn syrup. Cook over medium heat to the soft-ball stage, 235 degrees. Remove from heat and beat in butter and vanilla with a wooden spoon. Continue beating until mixture thickens. Drop by the tablespoonful onto waxed paper. Cool completely and store in air-tight container. Makes about 3 dozen.

Pat Shumard
Susan Provencher

▪ BUCKEYES ▪

3 pounds powdered sugar
2 pounds smooth peanut butter
1 pound butter **OR** margarine, softened
24 ounces chocolate chips
1 4-ounce bar paraffin wax

In a large bowl, combine powdered sugar, peanut butter and butter. Beat until smooth. Chill thoroughly. Form mixture into balls approximately 1-inch in diameter. Chill balls for 2 hours.

Melt the chocolate chips and paraffin together in the top of a double boiler over simmering water. Spear each ball with a toothpick and dip ¾ of the ball into the chocolate mixture. Place on a baking sheet covered with waxed paper to harden, then chill.

Helen Hall

CHILDREN

▪ THE DISCOVERY SPACE ▪

OMSI's Early Childhood Education Lab

The Discovery Space at OMSI opened it's doors in 1985. The staff envisioned a place where young minds could explore fine motor and gross motor skills, as well as tactile, visual, auditory and creative skills. Discovery Space has become not a playroom, not even a classroom, but much more. It is an area of our science museum completely devoted to the basic science all around us. Discovery Space is the science in a glass of air held upside down in water, or in a basic pulley system that allows the child to transport objects across a room crowded with other children. It is the science of movement in a pipe system where a little girl or boy places balls in one end and watches them plowing down through curves and corners, finally bouncing out on the other end into the bucket of an anxiously awaiting child.

But is this really science? The argument will always be heard that playing is indisputably an essential part of any child's growth process, but to call it science is absurd. Isn't science, after all, men and women in white lab coats standing around looking at test tubes? Looking back at my own high school classes in physics and chemistry, I certainly remember that my image of scientists was exactly that. It held me back, by making me think that unless I could perform complex experiments in chemistry, I could never call myself a scientist.

What a nightmare, and how unnecessary. Adults who bring their children to the Discovery Space today frequently tell us how they wish the Lab had been here during their own childhood. But they feel fortunate now that, they have the chance to watch how openly their children receive science when it is presented at an early age. So what about chemistry and physics? Can such advanced topics even begin to be explored with a child of three? You bet. Set up two cups of baking soda, and two squeeze bottles, one with water and one with vinegar. Stand back and let your child experiment. What happens? Two of the above ingredients combined makes bubbles. That is chemistry. Pure and simple. The child is working to provoke change in the materials she or he is using. Not only that, they figure it out all on their own, and you can bet that if your child keeps playing like this, high school science will be a breeze.

Our new Discovery Space continues building on this philosophy. We offer the Kid Chemistry Lab, where experiments such as the one above continue everyday, all day. Have you heard of Flubber? That's one of our specialties, available one week a month in the Lab. Next to Kid Chemistry we have WaterWorks, where children can experiment with water play in an innovative water pump table. We also have an amazing Mechanics Deck and many physics activities tied to it, by way of creating, changing, and observing movement with balls, pulleys, inclines, cranes and simple machines.

We have live animals in our nature lab; mice, parakeets, and a four-foot boa constrictor named Ginger. Children have a chance to touch the boa and see how gentle she is. They can also come back at feeding time and watch her as she feeds on a small mouse. Last and perhaps most importantly, we offer an entire area to parents with newborn babies and children up to two years old. This space is soft, safe and a little quieter than anywhere else.

We always welcome support from the community both financially and through volunteers. We intend to keep working for further understanding of how the young mind develops. But for now, we feel content to lay out the groundwork, then stand back and let children learn.

Laura Lundy-Paine
Early Childhood Education Specialist

▪ COPPER PLATING A NAIL ▪

You will need:

½ cup vinegar
½ teaspoon salt
A glass container
10 dull copper pennies (make sure that your pennies are dated before 1983 to get the best results)
1 iron nail

Mix the vinegar and salt together in the glass container. Add the dull pennies and leave them in the vinegar mixture until they become clean. Clean the iron nail very well with steel wool or abrasive cleanser and rinse thoroughly. Place the clean nail into the vinegar mixture. Let the nail stay in the solution for about 10 minutes. The nail will be covered with a bright coating of copper.

▪ HOT COCOA MIX ▪

3 cups non-fat dry milk
1 cup sugar
⅔ cup unsweetened cocoa powder
½ teaspoon salt

Mix all ingredients together with a fork until well blended. Store in an airtight container.

To make hot cocoa:

Add ¼ cup Hot Cocoa Mix and 1 cup boiling water and stir until smooth.

▪ CHOCOLATE COVERED PEANUTS ▪

1 18-ounce package chocolate chips
1 6-ounce package butterscotch chips
2 teaspoons paraffin wax, chopped
1 13-ounce can salted Spanish peanuts

In the top of a double-boiler, combine chocolate chips, butterscotch chips and paraffin, Melt over medium-low heat, stirring gently. Add in salted peanuts and stir to coat thoroughly. Drop by teaspoonfuls onto waxed paper. Allow to harden.

Nathan Whited

▪ PINE CONE BIRD FEEDERS ▪

Go to the woods and gather new-fallen pine cones. Pack loosely in a cardboard box, uncovered, and put in a dry place to cure.

After Christmas is over, move your tree outside to your porch. Leave the tree in the stand. Get the dry and now opened pine cones out of storage. Tie a 12-inch string tightly around the top of the pine cone so that the pine cone is in the middle of the string. Tie the ends of the string together so it will form a loop that you can hang on the branches of the Christmas tree.

Get a dull knife out of the drawer and spread lots of natural peanut butter all over the pine cone. Roll the pine cone in wild bird seed. Hang the pine cones in the Christmas tree.

Get Dad to smash a suet ball on the very top of the Christmas tree.

Refill pine cones as needed.

Brandon Poppert

Mealworms

Mealworms are a favorite food of many reptile pets such as iguanas, geckos and other lizards. You can grow your own mealworms instead of buying them regularly at the pet store.

You will need:

1 container of mealworms from the pet store
Gallon jar with wide mouth
Oatmeal or cornflake crumbs
Apple or potato slice
Crinkled up paper
Square of gauze or cotton cloth
Rubber band

Clean jar and dry it thoroughly. Put in enough oatmeal to fill 1/4 of the jar. Place one slice of apple in the jar. Add mealworms. Stretch the gauze or cotton cloth over the jar mouth and hold secure with the rubber band. When mealworms are in the pupa stage add the crinkled paper. When the pupa hatch into beetles they will crawl onto the crinkled paper.

Weekly care: Change the apple slice weekly since mold will kill the mealworms.

Cleaning: If any mold does grow, clean jar and change oatmeal as soon as possible.

Helpful Hints: Mealworms do best in a warm dark place such as a cupboard.

Gretchen Beth Snyder

▪ SCOTCHEROOS ▪

This recipe was a camping staple while I was growing up, and now I make them for my kids.

1 cup light corn syrup
1 cup sugar
1 cup peanut butter
7 cups Rice Krispies cereal
6 ounces butterscotch chips
6 ounces chocolate chips

In a medium sauce pan, stir together corn syrup and sugar. Bring to a boil, reduce heat to medium and simmer until sugar dissolves. Remove from heat and pour into a large bowl. Add peanut butter and blend well. Stir in Rice Krispies. Press mixture into a 9-inch by 13-inch by 2-inch pan.

Melt butterscotch chips and chocolate chips together in a double-boiler. Spread over top of Rice Krispie mixture. Cool, then cut into bars.

Renee White

▪ NO-BAKE BANANA COOKIES ▪

2 cups fine vanilla wafer crumbs
1/2 cup wheat germ
1/2 to 1 cup ripe bananas, mashed
1/4 cup coconut
Powdered sugar

Place vanilla wafer crumbs, wheat germ, mashed bananas and coconut in a large bowl. Mix with hands until well blended. Shape into 1-inch balls and roll in powdered sugar. Store in air-tight container in the refrigerator.

Jenny Long

▪ THE *BEST* PLAYDOUGH ▪

3 cups flour
1 1/2 cups salt
3 tablespoons cream of tartar
4 tablespoons oil
Food coloring
3 cups water

Mix flour, salt and cream of tartar together in a 2-quart sauce pan. Add oil and food coloring to water and stir into dry ingredients. What a lumpy, runny mess! About this time you are probably thinking there must be a mistake in this recipe, but please proceed. Cook over medium heat for about 5 minutes, stirring often. As soon as mixture begins to thicken and pull together into a ball, remove from heat. Place on floured board to cool slightly and then knead until smooth.

This takes only a few minutes to make and is well worth the time since it will last for several months if stored in and airtight container.

Sue Manning

"Imagineering" . . . What is it? Well, it's a cross between "imagination" and "engineering." It's the product of two endeavors that kids seem to be naturals at. Put them together and you've got the ingredients for a great afternoon of inventing!

▪ STICKY BISCUITS ▪

This is very easy to make, even if you are only eleven years old. I like to make these for my family and we like to snack on Sticky Biscuits.

¼ cup light corn syrup
¼ cup brown sugar
¼ cup chopped walnuts
1 can refrigerated biscuits

Preheat oven to 425 degrees.

Take out a round cake pan. Spread the corn syrup in the bottom. Sprinkle the brown sugar over the syrup. Sprinkle the walnuts over the brown sugar. Cut each refrigerator biscuit into 4 pieces. Place biscuit pieces on top of walnuts. Place in oven and bake for 10 minutes. After it is baked, remove pan from oven and invert the pan onto a plate so the sticky side is up. Serve immediately.

Nathan Adams

▪ CHRISTOPHER'S NEW SOUP ▪

I invented this recipe and it was voted best soup recipe in Miss Hardwick's 2nd grade class. Your Mom can help with the peeling and slicing.

10 carrots, peeled and sliced
5 potatoes, peeled and cut into 1-inch cubes
2 cups broccoli florets
2 cups corn
1 cup celery, sliced
10 cups water
5 chicken bouillon cubes
3 teaspoons salt

Place all ingredients in a large pot. Bring to a boil. Reduce heat to medium-low and simmer for about 30 minutes or until vegetables are tender.

Christopher Michael Provencher, age 8

▪ RECIPE FOR A CHOCOLATE MILKSHAKE ▪

¾ cup 2% milk
3 tablespoons chocolate syrup
1 pint vanilla frozen yogurt

Pour milk into a blender container. Add chocolate syrup. Cover and blend on low speed until smooth. Add half of the frozen yogurt. Cover and blend on low speed until smooth. Add remaining frozen yogurt. Cover and blend on low until smooth. Makes two milkshakes.

Matthew G. Provencher

Dinosaur Stew

1 medium dinosaur
Brown gravy
Salt and pepper to taste
2 rabbits

Cut dinosaur into bite-sized pieces. This should take about two months. Add enough brown gravy to cover. Season with salt and pepper. Cook over a charcoal fire for about 4 weeks at 475 degrees.

This recipe will serve 3,000 people. If more are expected, 2 rabbits may be added. Do this only if absolutely necessary; most people do not like to find hare in their stew.

▪ INK TEST ▪

(PAPER CHROMATOGRAPHY)

You will need:

A plastic trough or other shallow container
Wooden dowel long enough to suspend it over the sides of the trough
Paper towels
Masking tape
Colored felt pens

Set out the ink test trough with about 1½-inches water in the bottom. Cut up the paper towels into 1-inch by 4-inch strips.

1. Tape the narrow end of one of the paper strips to a wooden dowel.
2. Suspend it from the sides of the trough so that the end of the paper touches the water.
3. Pick out a felt pen to test.
4. Remove the paper from the water and draw a line across it with the felt pen, just above the waterline.
5. Suspend the paper in the trough again and wait for a little while. The water will move up the paper, separating the ink into the colors it was made from.

Capillary action causes the water to rise up the strip of paper towel. As is rises, lighter inks rise faster than the heavier inks, and you can see all of the component pigments of the felt pen.

Bill Hanshumaker

▪ SOAP TEST ▪

You will need:
Graduated cylinder
for measuring
2 large (8" x 1") test tubes
with rubber stoppers
1 test tube rack
Water
Vegetable oil
Dishwashing soap

1. Using the graduated cylinder, measure out 7 milliliters of water and pour it into test tube #1.
2. Repeat step 1 with test tube #2.
3. Add oil to the water in the two test tubes, up to the 12.5 ml mark.
4. Place a rubber stopper in the top of test tube #1 and shake it for a few seconds.
5. Place test tube #1 back in the test tube rack and let it sit for a minute or so. Do the oil and water stay mixed?
6. Add 5 drops of soap to test tube #2.
7. Place a rubber stopper securely in the top of test tube #2 and shake it for a few seconds.
8. Place test tube #2 back in the test tube rack and let it sit for a minute or so. What happens to the oil and water this time?

In test tube #1, the oil and water should have separated back out into two distinct layers after it was shaken. The oil and water in test tube #2, which you added soap to, should have remained mixed with tiny bubbles of oil spread throughout the water.

This is a good example of how soap works. Grease is what causes dirt to stick to our clothes, skin, dishes, etc. The oil is a form of grease. Soap works by reducing the surface tension of the water. This means that the water molecules are not as attracted to each other as before. Therefore, they are more attracted to the grease molecules than they were before, enabling the grease to be washed away by water more easily. So you see, soap just helps clean. It wouldn't work without water.

Bill Hanshumaker

Discovery Space Quotes from Laura Lundy-Paine

The first question the teacher should ask is, "Will my question to the child enhance or detract from the child's exploration?" Usually an actively engaged child in a well-designed environment will benefit most by not being distracted by questions.

---*from The Young Child as Scientist, by Christine Chaille and Lory Britain.*

* * *

Children are theory builders as they construct an understanding of print, figure out the meaning of numbers and how they relate to objects, try different colors on the easel, interact with their friends, and figure out the meaning of reciprocity in friendship. Science in this very broad sense underlies the construction of all knowledge.

---*from The Young Child as Scientist, by Christine Chaille and Lory Britain.*

* * *

Don't forget to carry a few spare ideas along just in case the ones you selected fail without warning.

Don Kloberg & Jim Bagnell

* * *

Imagination is more important than knowledge.

Albert Einstein

* * *

. . . A good method for facilitating continuity is to teach children how to ask their own questions.

George Forman & David Kuschner

* * *

. . . The kind of experimental background in children's lives before schooling begins, or along the way, is more uniformly adequate to math and science than to most other school subjects.

David Hawkins

▪ GLUEP ▪

Before you make this cool concoction, be sure that you read through the directions with an adult and that you clean up your mess when you are finished!

2 tablespoons of white glue (like Elmers)
2 tablespoons water
1 or 2 drops food coloring
1 teaspoon Borax (powder)
⅓ cup water

Put glue and 2 tablespoons water in a disposable cup. Add food coloring and mix. In a separate container, combine Borax and ⅓ cup water and stir to dissolve. Slowly pour borax mixture into glue mixture while stirring with a popsicle stick or the disposable stirrer. If the Gluep doesn't all clump up on the stick, then add some more Borax and water.

Store your Gluep in a plastic zip-lock baggie. Don't leave Gluep on a wood surface or it will leave a mark.

OMSI Outreach Staff

▪ OOBLECK ▪

Remember the Dr. Seuss story "Bartholomew and the Oobleck"? Well, here's your chance to mix up your own batch of that weird green goo!

1 cup cornstarch
½ cup water, approximately
Food coloring (optional)

Put the cornstarch into a pie tin or other container. Add a drop or two of food coloring to the water. Add the water slowly to the cornstarch while mixing constantly. Be careful not to add too much water.

When you are done playing with the Oobleck, you may wash it down the sink with lots and lots of water.

David Heil
Newton's Apple
Associate Director, OMSI

▪ MOLD GARDEN ▪

1 orange
1 piece of bread
1 piece of cheese

Place each ingredient in a separate clean dish. Add a few drops of water to each dish and cover with plastic wrap. Place dishes in a dark place, such as a kitchen cabinet, for about a week. Take out the dishes when mold starts to grow on the food. Examine the molds with a magnifying glass. See how many different types and colors of mold have grown on the different foods. What else in the house will grow molds?

Do not try this experiment if you have an allergy to molds.

David Heil
Newton's Apple
Associate Director, OMSI

▪ FLUBBER ▪

This is HUGELY popular! Let the children participate in the measuring, pouring, mixing and kneading of the Flubber. Before you make this cool concoction, be sure that you read through the directions with an adult and that you clean up your mess when you are finished!

2 cups Elmer's White Glue
1½ cups warm water
Food coloring (if desired)
3 teaspoons Borax
1⅓ cups warm water

In a large bowl, blend glue and 1½ cups warm water. Add a few drops of food coloring if desired. In a separate large bowl, combine Borax with 1⅓ cups warm water and stir to dissolve.

Pour glue mixture into Borax mixture. Immediately get your hands in and start kneading the Flubber into shape. Lift the Flubber out of the water/borax bowl and place in other bowl. There will be a large amount of water left in the water/borax bowl which is to be discarded.

The Flubber can now be played with! Have a variety of small toys with different shapes and textures to press into the Flubber. Cookie cutters also work well.

When finished playing, store Flubber in an air-tight container. It lasts a week or so, depending on the amount of color used. Too much color, or color from ink pens, separates from Flubber and creates a mess in storage.

Laura Lundy Paine

Encouraging Imagineering in Children

Assemble a junk collection and a safe place to work

Help distinguish between function and ornamentation in inventions

Avoid saying "This won't work"

Remember where ownership lies . . . with the inventor!

Encourage creative thinking by promoting and rewarding

Originality	Fluency	Curiosity	Imagination
Elaboration	Flexibility	Complexity	Risk-taking

Have fun and promote humor as creative expression

Encourage persistence and patience

Celebrate the process as well as the product

David Heil
Newton's Apple
Associate Director, OMSI

▪ EGG DEELIES ▪

1 slice bread
1 tablespoon butter
1 egg

Cut a 2-inch hole in the center of the bread. Save the center cut-out.

Heat butter in a small skillet over medium-low heat. When the butter has melted, put the bread in the pan. Crack the egg into the hole in the bread. Cook until the bread is golden brown and the egg is partially set. Carefully turn over bread and egg with a spatula, taking care not to break the yolk. Cook until desired doneness. Serve with the center cut-out to dip into the yolk. Serves 1.

Mary Ingham
Stephen Ingham

▪ BUBBLE MIXTURE ▪

2 tablespoons liquid
dishwashing detergent
1 cup warm water

Gently stir together the detergent and water until well mixed. Let the Bubble Mixture stand overnight. Put into clean jars and use to blow bubbles.

▪ ROCK CANDY ▪

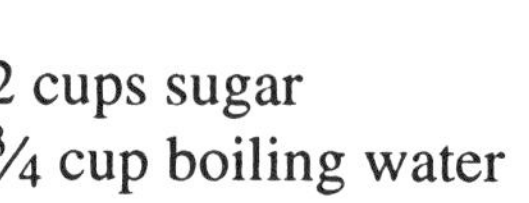

2 cups sugar
¾ cup boiling water

Dissolve sugar in boiling water. Pour syrup into a shallow dish. Set aside dish where it won't be disturbed. In about a week the water will have evaporated and the sugar crystals will form.

Dancing Raisins

Pour a glass of mineral water or light-colored soda pop. Add a few raisins and watch them dance in the glass! The carbon dioxide bubbles cling to the raisins and carry them up and down.

DOGS

▪ THE OMSI SCIENCE STORE ▪
"Finding Recipes for Imagination"

"Anyone who stops learning is old, whether at twenty or eighty. Anyone who keeps learning stays young. The greatest thing in life is to keep your mind young."
Henry Ford

The OMSI Science Store is both a celebration and a tradition of learning and discovery in Portland, Oregon, and is one of the oldest continuously-operating stores dedicated to science and science education in the Pacific Northwest. Owned and operated by the museum, it's mission—"to improve the public's understanding of science and technology"—is the essence of OMSI's mission statement. At any given time, the OMSI Science Store reflects OMSI's current interests in exhibits and programming, as well as the broader perspectives of science and technology taken as a whole.

Starting modestly in 1957 as a single used glass case housing gyroscopes and some educational souvenirs, the OMSI Science Store has grown over the years to encompass nearly 3,000 square feet of public sales space, and 1,500 square feet of support area. The OMSI Science Store's national reputation is built primarily on it's excellent selection of hands-on experiment books and kits, and for the uniformly high quality of it's optical equipment, primarily telescopes and microscopes. Visitors will also find a great selection of educational games and toys for people of all ages, plus posters, apparel, videos, computer programs, audio tapes and CDs, slides, models and basic laboratory supplies, mineral and meteorite specimens, and reference and enrichment books.

Not as well known as the main OMSI Science Store are it's wholesale and mail order operations. OMSI wholesales selected merchandise to commercial stores in the region, and to other museums throughout North America. Also, most of the materials the OMSI Science Store offers can be easily purchased by mail. In fact, many of OMSI Science Store's customers live well outside of the immediate Portland area, shopping routinely from as far away as Alaska, Michigan and Texas. International customers have included people in Japan, Australia, Venezuela and Israel.

One of the late Albert Einstein's best-known quotes was, "Imagination is more important than Knowledge", and the OMSI Science Store celebrates that idea with materials representing such popular OMSI exhibits as "SUPER HEROES®" and "STAR TREK: Federation Science™, perhaps not *wholly* today's hard science fact, but stellar launching points that take what we know today and explore what tomorrow's science fact *might* be like. The OMSI Science Store staff also participates in various community events, and in special OMSI events such as the annual "Winter Solstice", playfully turning the scientific clock *backwards* once a year to the 15th century!

In short, the OMSI Science Store is one of the museum's best ambassadors to the many audiences that look to OMSI. It not only reflects the museum's diversity of exhibits and programs, it celebrates the very essence of wonder and discovery that is science. Open free to the public all museum hours, the OMSI Science Store is rapidly becoming a visitor and shopping destination site in it's own right in metropolitan Portland.

Terry Hiller

If you feed the following complete diet to your dog (Dog Food, Oil Mix and Powder Supplement), it will repel fleas.

▪ A DOG FOOD RECIPE ▪

3 pounds ground turkey **OR** ground chicken
2 pounds short grain brown rice
1 pound pearl barley
1 pound green split peas
3 carrots, finely chopped
3 zucchini, finely chopped
5 cloves garlic, minced
Water to cover

Mix all ingredients together in a large pot. Bring to a boil, then reduce heat to low, cover, and simmer 1½ to 2 hours or until cooked. Check occasionally to see if more water is needed. Cool and refrigerate until needed. Feed approximately 2 cups dog food twice a day for a 55 to 60 pound dog. Ask your veterinarian about daily supplements.

Doran L. Whipple

▪ DOG OIL MIX ▪

(A NUTRITIONAL SUPPLEMENT)

Mix equal parts of olive oil and safflower oil. Keep in a dark cupboard.

Daily Dose:

Small Dog	Medium Dog	Large Dog
2 teaspoons	4 teaspoons	2 tablespoons

Doran L. Whipple

▪ DOG POWDER SUPPLEMENT MIX ▪

2 cups nutritional brewers yeast
1½ cups bone meal
½ cup kelp powder

Blend ingredients together. Store in an airtight container in a cool, dark place.

Weight of Dog	Daily Dose
5 to 15 pounds	2 teaspoons
15 to 30 pounds	4 teaspoons
30 to 50 pounds	2 tablespoons
50 to 100 pounds	3 tablespoons

Doran L. Whipple

▪ DOG BISCUITS ▪

3 cups stone-ground whole wheat flour
1 cup bran flakes
1 cup cornmeal
1 cup soya flour **OR** rye flour
1 cup wheat germ
1 cup sunflower seeds, ground
1 cup non-fat milk (low sodium)
1 tablespoon active dry yeast
1 egg
3¾ cups water **OR** vegetable broth
¼ cup olive oil **OR** safflower oil
1 teaspoon garlic powder

Preheat oven to 325 degrees. Oil baking sheets.

Combine all ingredients in a large bowl and blend well. Roll or pat out on lightly floured surface to ¼-inch to ½-inch thick. Cut into strips 1-inch by 3-inches, or use bone shaped cutter. Place on prepared baking sheets and bake for 1 hour. Turn off heat and leave biscuits in the oven overnight to harden. Store in an airtight container. Makes about 24 biscuits.

Barbara O'Connor

INDEX

▪ Young Scholars Research Program ▪

Made possible by a grant from the National Science Foundation, OMSI's Young Scholar's Program gives high school aged students with strong interests and abilities in the sciences an opportunity to spend a summer conducting research. Working under the supervision of professional researchers in either paleontology/geology, fisheries/freshwater ecology, or desert ecology, the 10 students in each team make meaningful contributions to on-going research efforts through field and lab studies. In addition to information and skills specific to each research team, students gain experience in problem-solving and scientific methods, as well as exposure to the philosophy of science and ethical issues relevant to scientific research. Participation in the research teams is available at no expense to the 30 participants who are selected from a large national field of applicants.

Connie Hofferber Jones

INDEX

C

D

J

K

L

M

N

O

P

Q

R

S

T

U

V

W

Y

USA
NASA
Challenger